marie claire
Dress
SKINNY

PERFECTING YOUR STYLE, FLATTERING YOUR BODY, AND LOOKING FABULOUS

Joyce Corrigan

RUNNING PRESS
PHILADELPHIA · LONDON

MARIE CLAIRE: DRESS SKINNY

© 2014 Hearst Communications, Inc.

Published by Running Press,
A Member of the Perseus Books Group

Printed in China

Books published by Running Press are available at special discounts for bulk purchases in the United States by corporations, institutions, and other organizations. For more information, please contact the Special Markets Department at the Perseus Books Group, 2300 Chestnut Street, Suite 200, Philadelphia, PA 19103, or call (800) 810-4145, ext. 5000, or e-mail special.markets@perseusbooks.com.

ISBN 978-0-7624-5407-5
Library of Congress Control Number: 2014942722

E-BOOK ISBN 978-0-7624-5539-3

9 8 7 6 5 4 3 2 1
Digit on the right indicates the number of this printing

DESIGNER: *Wanyi Jiang*
PHOTO EDITOR: *Karina Dearwood*
EDITOR: *Cindy De La Hoz*
TYPOGRAPHY: *Graphik, Miller Banner, Miller Daily One, and Miller Display*

Running Press Book Publishers
2300 Chestnut Street
Philadelphia, PA 19103-4371

Visit us on the web!
www.runningpress.com

Contents

Everybody has *those* days.

Nothing seems to fit. You've tried everything on. Your entire closet is on the floor. The one key article of clothing that might actually work is at the dry cleaners or in the laundry. And you wonder, *How did all of these dreadful things end up in my closet in the first place?*

And then we all have our favorite dress—the one you always have a great time in. Or the perfect jacket—the one you wear to important meetings because it makes you feel powerful. Or the cherished pair of jeans you slip into every Saturday because you know you can be yourself in them. And you marvel at the beauty of getting it right.

What if you had a closet full of clothes that actually made you feel good about the way you look every day? Impossible, you say? That's what we set out to do when we sat down to create this book: help every woman build a wardrobe that makes her feel fabulous.

We gathered tips, tricks, wisdom, camouflage secrets, optical illusions, and the little bits of magic that create flattering shapes and proportions—plus insight from designers and industry insiders who know how women want to look and feel in their clothes. Because wearing a dress that makes you feel pretty or a jacket that makes you feel powerful should not be a happy accident. We all deserve to feel that spring in our step, that confidence that comes from getting it right. So that you can get on with the business of being yourself.

Introduction *by* Anne Fulenwider

Perfection *is* overrated—

especially when it comes to the human body. I am a firm believer that it's our imperfections that make us unique. Think about some of history's most iconic and beautiful women. Elizabeth Taylor and Sophia Loren never fit the traditional mold. Jennifer Lopez became famous for her curves. And today's most sought-after celebrities—Rihanna, Kate Upton, Salma Hayek, Kim Kardashian, Beyoncé—they're not model-thin and fashion designers of the highest caliber are practically begging to dress them.

Growing up, my mother was voluptuous but she always managed to make it look like getting dressed was effortless for her (and trust me, it wasn't). She played up her best qualities—a small waist and feminine décolletage—by wearing dresses and skirts and avoiding pants (which is practically the opposite of what I wear!). It was never about trying to look like the models in magazines or the actresses on the big screen. And I have always tried to apply the same rationale.

As women, our bodies are constantly changing—sometimes from month to month or even week to week. It's important for us to learn how to think in terms of proportion and understand what shapes, colors, and sizes work for us as individuals. Personally, I find that I am generally more comfortable in streamlined silhouettes. Hold the ruffles, pleats, ruching, and over-the-top draping for someone else. If you haven't quite figured out what exactly it is that works best for you, let *Dress Skinny* be your guide. My only rule? Accentuate the positive—because nothing looks good if you don't feel good.

Introduction *by* Nina Garcia

Dressing to Flatter
BOOBS

Take the plunge. Best-dressed breasts emerge from a dynamic mix of carefully picked colors, perfect proportions, and strategic necklines.

STACKED IN YOUR FAVOR

Gazingas, bazooms, hooters, puppies, mams. Boobs have always been front and center of Western culture, causing no end of, well, tittering among the chattering classes. A star's cleavage is front-page news whenever there's the slightest wardrobe malfunction. Considering their biological role, nothing else quite puts the fun in functional as breasts. And it's great to enjoy and flaunt yours, just don't let the joke be on you. Great style is born of confidence in knowing what works for your body. Perfect-fit clothes should skim, never squeeze. Neither should you hide a great bust under billowy clothes that only make you look supersized and shapeless. Keeping boobs in proportion to the rest of you goes a long way toward getting a sleek, chic modern look.

At times, of course, dressing breasts is all about undressing them. Corsets that pushed boobs into view were popularized by Catherine de Médici, the most powerful woman of the Renaissance; serious cleavage was a show of both sexual confidence and worldliness as it mimicked the naked classical goddess statues aristo women had seen in museums or traveling. The theme stuck: big-breasted stars from Sophia Loren to Sofía Vergara are known as sirens, after the sailor-seducing femmes fatales of Greek mythology. And while Marilyn Monroe certainly didn't need the boost, lacing into a corset for several movies certainly promoted her to all-time favorite pinup status. The sex/power association was sealed when, as legend has it, the broad-rimmed champagne glass was molded on Queen Marie-Antoinette's own breasts. *Á votre santé!* From Madonna's lethal-weapon cone bras of the '90s to Dita Von Teese's rank as reigning burlesque queen and lingerie mogul, the new sexy means being in control of your boobs. Extreme cleavage looks tacky, not confident or on trend. Dressy nights or beach days are fine for flaunting what you've got, but in the work place and other formal occasions, healthy discretion is advised. Otherwise you risk being upstaged by them. Balancing boobs with a dress, top, or bikini that supports and redistributes the bust will guarantee looking terrific, not top-heavy.

Clockwise from top left: Marilyn Monroe; Rosie Huntington-Whiteley; Dita Von Teese; Scarlett Johansson **Opposite page:** Sophia Loren

WORK IT

Professional situations call for being subtle about sexy assets: avoid midriffs and deep cleavage in the office and stick to blazers with small vertical lapels and a bit of shoulder pad that will elongate the torso. Vertical stripes will always create "length," too.

Two different curvy options: Concealing, as Jennifer Hudson does with a long-sleeved peplum or revealing like Zooey Deschanel's pale blue bustier.

12

Big-bosom buddies
1. Tie-front midriff
2. Shoulder-padded jacket
3. Abs-baring crop top
4. Sweetheart-neck bustier
5. Off-the-shoulder peplum
6. Scoop-neck pullover
7. Fitted bodice dress
8. Vertical lapel vest

1

2

3

4

5

6

7

8

allocate your
Assets

Soft bodies—not just skinny, hard ones—can look great in soft colors. As long as the shape is slimming, pastels paired with other pastels or neutrals can lighten up your whole look. Any top that's slightly snug around the waist and loosely skims or drapes the chest will affect a nice balance of proportions. Classic options include corsets, peplums, button-downs with darts, and tops that tie under the bust, thus visually equalizing the boobs and belly. Ditch fussy scarves, bows, or collar embellishments. Keep shoulders sharply defined with pads or nothing at all: Baring skin is a tried-and-tested trick for drawing the eye: so deep Vs, sleeveless and crop tops, and three-quarter sleeves visually "relieve" some of the weight on top.

Penélope Cruz
In the movie, *Broken Embraces*

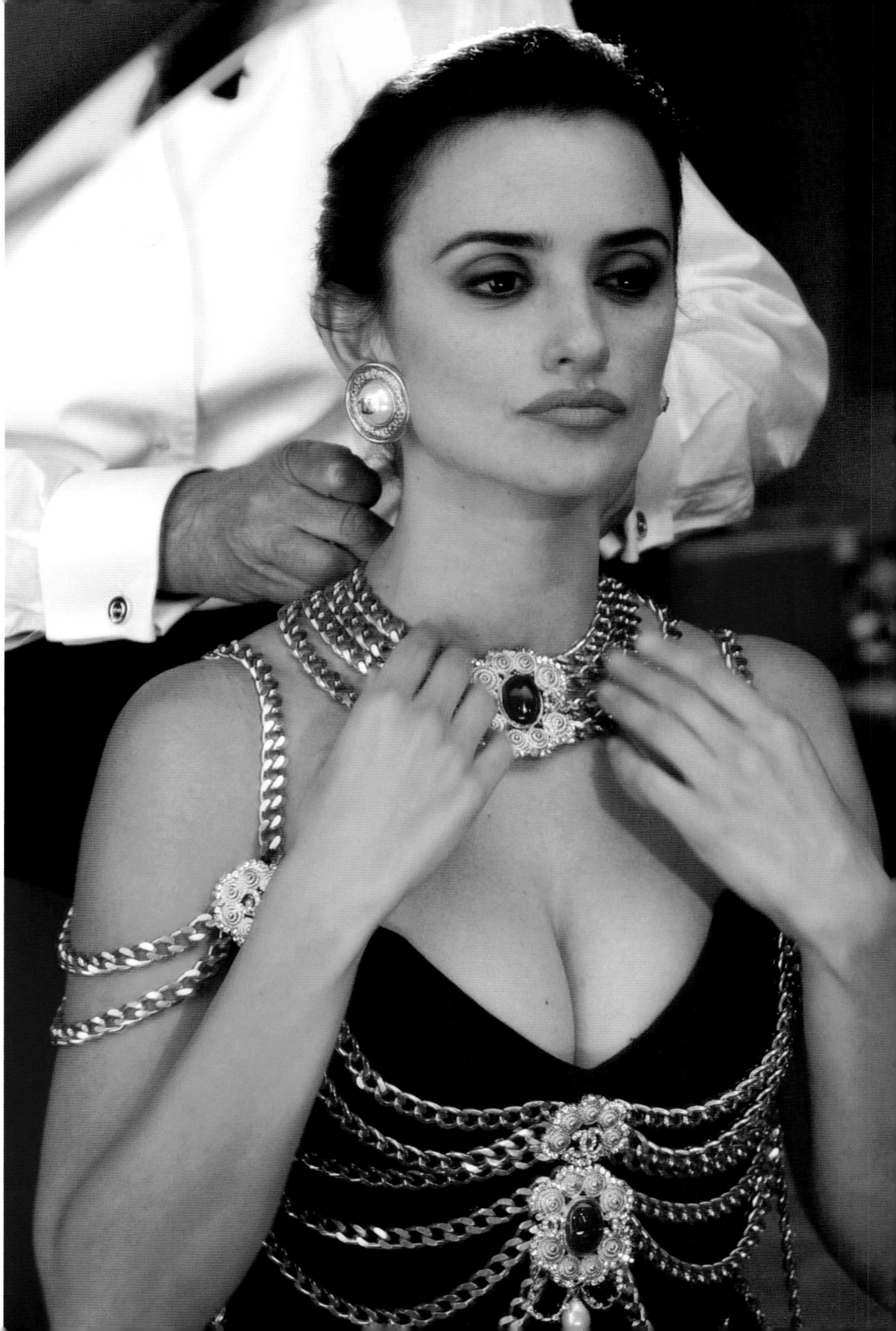

Catherine Zeta-Jones
Intolerable Cruelty

Natalie Dormer
Game of Thrones

Halle Berry
Introducing Dorothy Dandridge

1
2
3
4

"B" FOR BOMBSHELL

"I never do anything by chance," said '60s sex kitten Brigitte Bardot, and made it abundantly clear by the roles she took, the sweaters she wore, and the beehive she meticulously messed up. Screen sirens know this from seducing an audience and keeping it interested, and those with staying power never cross the line from bodacious to the butt of jokes. (Pamela Anderson's nipple mishap on *Dancing on Ice* ensures she won't be remembered for her tango, only her early exit.) So, learn from the legends: Stay classy. Invest in a good support system—namely, a dress or top with a well-cut neckline that exposes just enough, straps and sleeves that hold you up while showcasing shoulders, and a bra or bustier that reinforces your shape. Nothing so tight it squashes you and creates a boob-bulge visible under your blouse. Turn up the heat on your terms. Give it up for Sophia Loren who said: "Style must be adapted to the woman and not vice versa."

STYLE ARSENAL GLOSSARY

1. BUSTIER:
Corset-fitting, sleeveless top, with sturdy boning.

2. BALCONETTE BRA:
aka "shelf bra," padded, good for low-cut tops.

3. HALTER:
Supportive top that ties behind neck, built-in bra recommended.

4. SWEETHEART NECKLINE:
Scalloped-shaped low-cut neck that's high enough to cover bra cups.

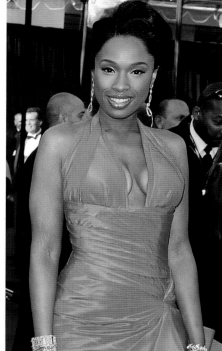

BALCONY VIEW

You'd be hard-pressed to find a more apt nickname for a big-bosomed babe than the French one—*"Il y'a du monde au balcon,"* which literally means "There's a crowd on the balcony." Without a parade of divas with décolleté gowns, there'd be no fans or paparazzi lining the red carpet, craning their necks for a better look at how low she did go! Of course, a precision-engineered party frock can make all the difference whether she's a hit or a flop. Fantasy and finesse, seduction and subtlety meet when the bosom is shown to its best advantage without compromising your peace of mind. Even if your workday look is all tailored and sharp-edged, go full-on feminine for dates. That said, if you're well-endowed, give functional and femme fatale equal time. What stands between you and looking like a star are tough decisions. First choose fabrics like satin, taffeta, lace, and chiffon (as long as it's lined) that are fluid and figure skimming but not too flimsy. *Marie Claire* columnist Nicollette Mason talks about the magic of gathered fabrics: "Ruching or draping at the bust is a clever design trick—it enlarges those who need it while minimizing those who don't." Luxury materials that elegantly contour or hint at curves are the savvy choice. Expensive? Probably, but since you've tossed most things from your trendista days, you've got room for wearable investments that work for you and will last. A scoop or plunging neckline will visually lengthen the neck and make you look taller, while a sweetheart or square neck that offers an expanse of bare flesh between your arms will also make you look lighter. Bare arms are your best bet, too, in that while catching the eye, they also alleviate the heft up top. Strapless isn't off limits, providing you have invisible support like a shapewear bra or corset with a built-in strapless bra to prevent sagging.

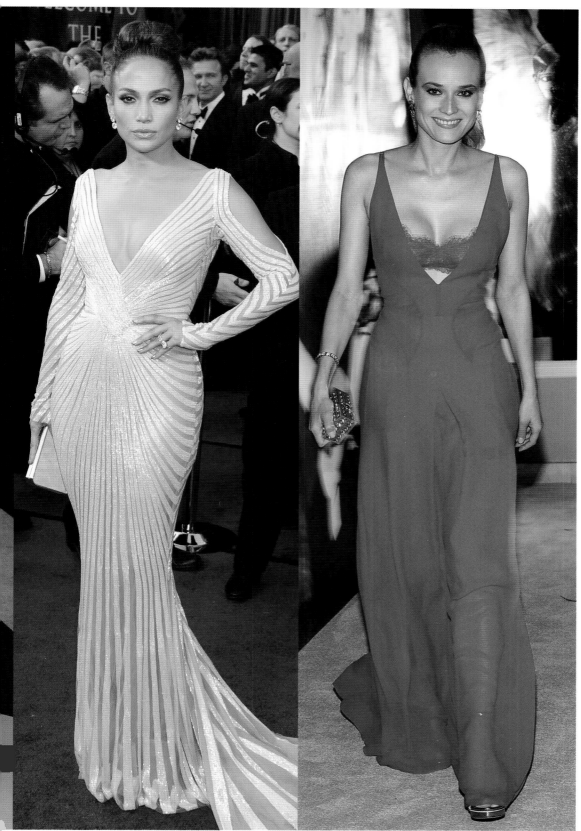

BATHING SUITS: TREASURE CHESTS

"The bikini is the most important thing since the atomic bomb," Diana Vreeland once decreed, and certainly the tiny, titillating two-piece was nothing if not a game changer—a way to flaunt your charms in public in an almost-acceptable way. But skimpy swimwear also puts pressure on the well-endowed: if it doesn't fit, the oceanfront knows it. That's where engineering comes in: from two-pieces with sweetheart necks and boyshort bottoms to swim-team style tanks with eye-catching high-cut legs to one-piece prints that strategically slim the silhouette.

Babe watch
Liz Taylor in a gleaming halter one-piece with built-in bra support

2
Heart this!
The classic scallop-shaped sweetheart top and retro highwaist bottom hit all the hot spots.

1
Print it
Minimize a large bust with dark colors and patterns up top and light ones elsewhere.

COVER-UP GIRLS
Far left: Kim Kardashian creates contours with a skinny belt; Left, a streamlined tank and trackpant make a good team.

3
Ruche it
A one-shoulder gathered maillot manipulates the eyes of the beholder so they're not locked on boobs.

GET THE LOOK

Precisely because your bust is often the first thing people notice is why you want to take care dressing the rest of you. Great style is about diversion tactics, no matter what your size or figure. That means steering the eye to what you want to show off and away from the rest. And when handling those most dangerous curves—your boobs—you want to be in the driver's seat. The goal is getting your top-to-toe look in proportion. Whether the season's trends are ultralean or voluminous, feminine, and flouncy, or boyish and boxy, it's up to you to tailor your outfit to your body. It should go without saying that a dress that's spot-on perfect on your best friend may fit you like a sack of Idaho potatoes—even if you're the same dress size! If big boobs are your style issue, your goal is to visually balance them out. Starting from the top, cause a little commotion with stunning collars and necklines. A brightly colored face-framing fur collar or shoulder embellishment can do the trick as long as it's not too fussy, which will just add "weight." Nothing quite adjusts proportion as powerfully as a plunging scoop or deep V neckline that optically lengthens the torso simply by baring skin.

Big-breasted girls should mind their torsos, too—as in don't try to disguise your endowment with a free-flowing top or dress. You'll look like a clipper ship at full sail. Instead, select nipped waist shirts, corset tops, and wrap dresses and coats that can be loosely belted, creating an hourglass with a fluid or full skirt below.

Prefer pants? Wide-legged trousers with a tailored top can carve out the same slim shape. There's no perfect palette for downsizing your silhouette but in general, dark colors on top worn with light-colored bottoms will minimize your bust. A solid-colored dress—the longer the better—creates one long, lean unbroken line.

And don't forget the power of naked. Use it sparingly at work, but whenever possible, bare shoulders, arms, and legs will literally "air out" your whole look.

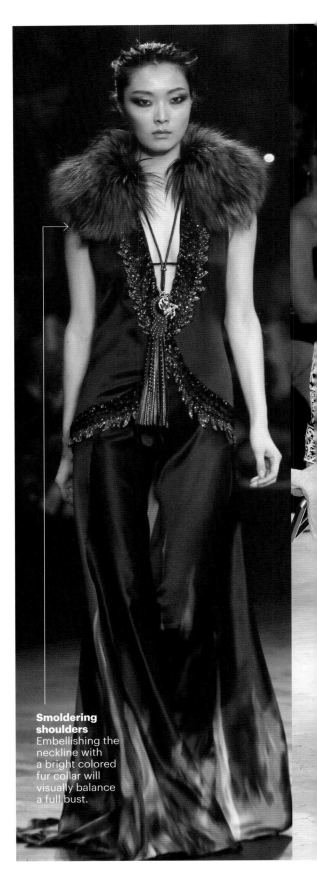

Smoldering shoulders Embellishing the neckline with a bright colored fur collar will visually balance a full bust.

Wrap it up
A loosely belted coat creates a a sleek hourglass silhouette, which is far more slimming than a shapeless, boxy coat.

Peasant uprising
The full-gathered peasant sleeve offsets the prominent bust of a peasant dress's low-cut scoop and corset shape.

Bare necessity
A novelty neckline, such as this quasi-superhero V shape, is eye-catching and more newsworthy than nude.

STREET STYLE: UPFRONT

Life's real runway is the street, where we see trends translated into the most truly wearable looks. Here, women who've learned to play to their strengths excel at being both inventive and chic. Enjoy these pointers about flattering a full bust from a pantheon of very polished city girls.

Dark monochrome top contrasted with light, graphic pants streamlines the top while putting legs in the spotlight. Long sleeves pushed up to show skin lightens up the look.

An off-the-shoulder neckline, aka the Carmen, referencing its flamenco roots, draws all eyes to neck and shoulder, while balloon sleeves balance out the bustline.

A simple but unusual neckline, like a big bib, acts like a statement necklace and creates a distraction. It also "breaks up" what could be the monotony of a large all-white surface.

Long and tall in a jumpsuit
While the dark monochrome suit creates an unbroken line, the ruffle wrap top visually separates boobs, diminishing the appearance of a "shelf."

Vixenish V
Like a downward arrow, deep V necklines lure the eye to parts beyond the bust, enabling the curviest bodies to look good in the busiest prints.

Give the bold shoulder, with a superwide V neck. Off-the-shoulder straps, supersized silver pendant, and zebra stilettos elevate this LBD with a little tribal intrigue.

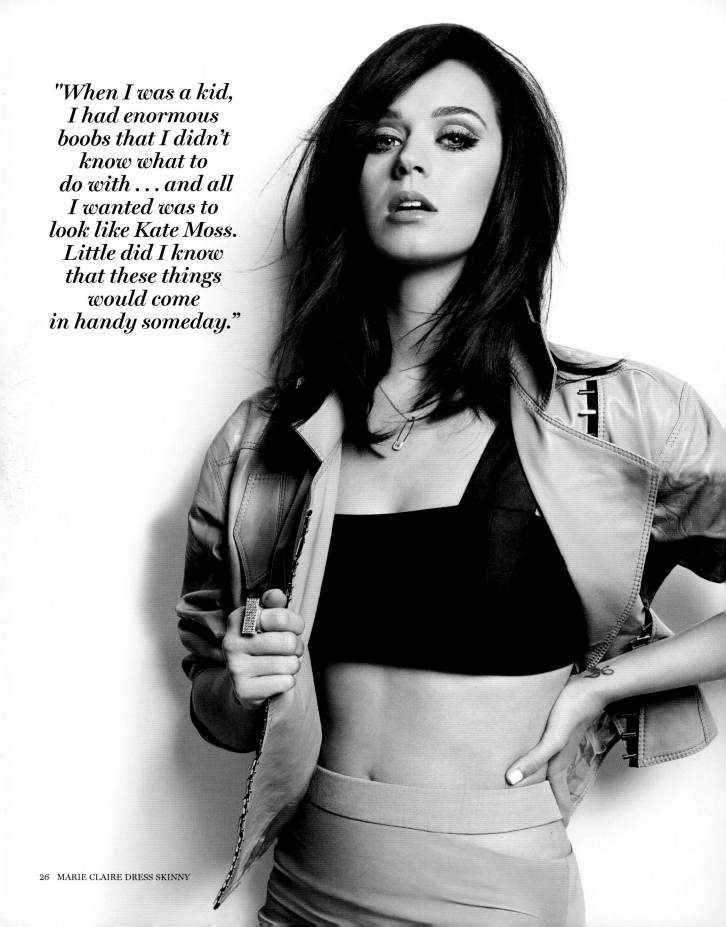

"When I was a kid, I had enormous boobs that I didn't know what to do with . . . and all I wanted was to look like Kate Moss. Little did I know that these things would come in handy someday."

KATY PERRY

With her superpowerful pipes and acclaimed curves, Katy Perry has become one of the red carpet's most sensational young stars. Her electrifying appearances onstage at awards shows or movie premieres are among the most anticipated as her fashion choices are sexy, original, and risk-taking, swinging from retro Hollywood to frilly girl to futuristic space age. While her cutie-pie face and Barbie body could consign her to purely pinup status, she goes where most pop divas fear to tread. But becoming pitch-perfect style-wise took years of trial and error. Perry wasn't born with body confidence, she acquired it. As a 5'7", 145-pound teenager, she had enormous breasts that she didn't know what to do with, so she downplayed them. "I wore minimizers, which were not cute," she recalls "Those thick-ass straps! I got made fun of for the over-the-shoulder boulder holder." Her wish was to be waifish, like prevailing supermodels; it was only after she'd grown into her talent and her career took off that she finally, as the song goes, let her colors burst.

"Mine isn't a Kate Moss body, but I'm very happy with it," she's said. Her greatest fashion hits (illustrated below) prove the point. Among them are: the red velvet fit-and-flare frock by Dolce & Gabbana whose ruched, bust-sculpting sweetheart neckline is balanced out by a full skirt. At the 2009 Grammys she rocked another perfectly proportioned number: a frothy pink strapless. The Basil Soda gown with bejeweled bow at the waist and a slenderizing pleated skirt. Like a modern fairy tale with an empowering message: the sparkling mermaid dress with supersized scoop neck is gracefully offset by a sheer flounce.

Her "If you risk nothing, you risk everything" approach to both her style and her music has paid off: "I don't care what people say about my boobs. People are buying my songs. I have a sold-out tour."

BEST OF KATY'S STYLE
Key to the pop star's red carpet look: keeping all parts in harmony.

1. Necklines swing lo'
From sweethearts to scoops to deep Vs, Katy shows off the depth of her famous charms.

2. Baring arms
Katy's toned arms are more than cut out for sleeveless gowns, high-collar halters, and skinny straps. The secret? A good bra as backup!

3. Flirty skirts
With all the dancing she does, no wonder she shows her legs with the occasional short, formal frock. Full skirts, flouncy hems, poufs, and mermaid flares all bring her big bust into proportion.

27

Ask Diane

(Ms. von Furstenberg weighs in on curves.)

The woman who put American women back in dresses dishes about corsets, halters, and her signature "wrap"—which 40 years on is sexier than ever.

Madonna

Oprah

Before she was the designer whom *Newsweek* dubbed "the most marketable female in fashion since Coco Chanel," Diane von Furstenberg was an ambitious young working woman in need of clothes to take her where she wanted to go. Thus was born her slinky, jersey wrap dress, which slips on and off with ease between office and evening-out and then emerges wrinkle free from a suitcase. Simple, slimming, sexy, the real magic is in the malleability: The wrap flatters figures from size 0 to 20. It's the Everywoman dress. "When Madonna wants to play down who she is and just be herself, she wears DVF," says DVF! This object of desire was inspired by the cozy, cropped wrap sweaters ballerinas wear in rehearsal, which Diane partnered with a graceful, fluid skirt. Forty years on, the robe-like wrap is just hitting its stride.

How does the wrap dress help a well-endowed girl balance her whole look?
DVF: The wrap dress is all about body language . . . the silk jersey fabric is close to the body without being clingy. It flatters the bust and has just enough stretch and a self-tie waist to hold you in. It's really effortless.

Halters and corset tops can hit or miss depending on the figure. What advice do you have for full-figured girls?
DVF: I think corsets are great and very of the moment. A curvier woman will want to balance the top with a fuller skirt, to achieve a nice proportion. Halters can be more complicated; you need to choose one with structure.

Any advice for using prints to your advantage, say highlighting certain curves and downplaying others?
DVF: Animal prints are best. They're fun and feline and move with the body, accentuating all of the right curves. High-contrast florals and abstract prints all have movement that can't help but catch the eye.

Dressing to Flatter
ARMS

Muscle in on the vast range of arm-enhancing options from off the shoulder to off the cuff.

Elbow room
Jackie looking oh so chic in sleeveless; cape crusader Zhang Lanxin; Beyoncé in arms-molding mesh sleeves; Talyor Swift, poised in a sheer peasant top.

BABE IN ARMS

Nudes aside, bare female arms barely showed up in paintings—much less in public—much before the twentieth century. While low-cut dresses afforded boobs almost complete exposure, sleeves came in one length: long. It wasn't until 1890 that Frances Cleveland, the much-younger wife of President Cleveland, dared wear a sleeveless gown to an official function. The Women's Christian Temperance Union cried "foul," but the First Lady wouldn't cave and waved in a trend that subsequent FLOTUSes like Jackie O and Michelle Obama have taken and run with. Once women flexed their muscles at work, in sports, and onstage, confining clothes no longer cut it. Short sleeves and sleeveless are now style staples for both work and play. Naturally, while having the right to bare arms, you can also exercise the option to minimize, conceal, or accessorize them to your best advantage. An excellent evening option is a sexy off-the-shoulder style with a neckline that bares the smooth, angular shoulder zone and sleeves or straps that cover just the upper arms. And sheer up: whether red carpet ready in mesh organza sleeves or beach bound in see-through cotton peasant tops, you're provocative but protected with see-through materials. So demo your newfound arms confidence! Think skinny girls never stress about arms? It was model icon Twiggy who once waxed poetic about a long flared sleeve: "It's a great way to distract from the dreaded bingo wings."

Baring it Italian-style
Neopolitan diva Sophia Loren in upper-arm flattering '50s fit and flare.

FIT TO PRINT
Abstract design plus three-quarter sleeve equals slender look.

Beyond measure
Sleeves that shave inches:
1. Kimono shirt dress
2. Crocheted peasant
3. Striped shawl
4. Three-quarter puff
5. Diaphanous shirt sleeve
6. Quilted sleeve moto
7. Floral raglan top

Armed forces
A cropped top with full cap sleeve, above, creates air between skin and sleeve, skinnifying the arm; Curvy Kate Winslet's sparkly one-shoulder lures eyes to her face; A sleeveless Gucci gown with a flourish of coverup thanks to a a blue floral-embroidered shrug; Bell of the ball, right, with a long fit-and-flare bell sleeve.

1

2

3

4

allocate your
Assets

Get a grip on glamour by choosing bold statement sleeves that selectively reveal only leanest sections. From funnel-like kimono sleeves to gathered peasant styles to puffs, there's no end to sleeves that bring a little dash to a dress or top while cleverly concealing upper limbs. Just because your arms are covered doesn't mean your look can't feel fresh and light: brighten it up with neon colors, romantic florals, sheer chiffon sleeves, or craftsy crochets.

7

6

5

ASIA MAJOR
*Tibetan-inspired
crisscross
vest constructs a
sharp look
for shoulders.*

TOUCHY
*A multitexture solid
dress with "no-
shoulder" raglan
sleeve affects a long,
lean line
from collar to hem.*

**RAGLAN TO
RICHES**
*Seamless raglan
cap sleeves in
pastel fur give
upper arms the
posh treatment.*

HANG LOOSE
*The kaftan's
long robe shape
says relaxed; the
splendidly wide
patterned sleeves
say regal.*

DRESSES

How easy it is to miss the mark with an otherwise fab dress that's undermined by too tight or too short sleeves. Target only your leanest bits—shoulders, forearms, wrists—and camouflage the rest.

Play up shoulders
Flaunt the fittest parts of your arm: from left to right: short and sweet, cutout and cropped, long and lacy, wild and ruffled.

TOPS & JACKETS

The trick to sleek-looking arms is a topper with tactical sleeves and armholes. Ensure visible space between your skin and sleeves and arms will always look leaner. Raves for raglan sleeves, that extend from the collar to cuff creating the illusion of a long, slim line. Ditto dolman sleeves that swoop low underneath. Wear smart on your sleeve: make sure they end just below your fleshiest no-show zone and avoid fabric extremes: skin tight and clingy will broadcast any bulges, while super stiff will only amplify your natural contour.

FRONT LINE
Contrast stripes that engulf arms clearly compress width.

RIPPLE EFFECT
Splashy prints wear art on short sleeves.

SALUTE!
Kickass military jacket with arm-slimming black sleeves.

CHILL CHASER
Megasize muffler keeps you warm and your arms looking undeniably hot.

BIG SHRUG
Bright color fur boleros, left and right, assure lots of luxe while covering upper limbs.

GOT SPOTS?
A diaphanous dot-print shawl is more than merely pretty: graphics give it edge.

PASHMINA MINE
Once the domain of the terminally prim, upper body-sheltering shawls have gone hip.

SHRUGS & SHAWLS

The supersized scarf, aka the shawl, is a strong-armed girl's godsend: a fashionable pop of color but also serving a dual purpose of keeping chill at bay and embellishing arms. For glam summer nights, a gossamer fabric like chiffon or georgette conceals without overwhelming your frock. For winter affairs, vibrant pashminas and colorful fur scarves—could there be a more posh accent? When you can no longer resist that sexy sleeveless shift, slip into a short-sleeved shrug.

Sheer madness
Ballsy belles of the ball, Kelly Osbourne and Mindy Kaling flirt with fanfare via jeweled embroidery and a riot of organza ruffles.

REACH FOR THE STARS

Modern women who've elbowed their way to the top don't skimp when it comes to big-impact looks for the limelight. Whether model-thin like Alexa Chung or famously fleshy like funny girl Lena Dunham, their fashion choices reveal a keen awareness of their bodies as well as a penchant for taking attention-getting risks. (Would Lena's off-the-shoulder frocks pack as much punch if she weren't sporting tough-chick tats on her upper arm?") Anatomically speaking, arms and boobs stand together, so it's always wise to consider the two when choosing styles. Necklines that flatter big boobs—V necks, scoops, and sweethearts—will also draw the eye to the neck and away from the upper arm. Maximum embellishments like a sheer lace bodice or organza ruffle necklines are consummate scene stealers, ensuring the eye is locked on them and not on areas you'd rather keep in the wings. And whether dressing red carpet or super casual, think like a techie: colorize areas you want to flaunt with brights and graphics and minimize those you don't.

Clockwise from top left: Alexa Chung's cape dress; Lena's off-the-shoulder gown; Ginnifer Goodwin's pink bell sleeves; Zoë Kravitz's drop-shoulder romper.

In neutral
Rita Ora's low-cut kimono sleeve dress has it made in the shade.

Peek performance
Lupita Nyong'o's riveting red cape dress reinterprets Romanticism.

Bold shoulder
Mrs. Obama dons a one-shoulder goddess gown parading her divinely toned limbs.

Peasant day
Chiffon and silk lavished with sequins give Leighton Meester's peasant top an upgrade.

ARMS OF AN ANGEL

Nothing packs a punch quite like a pair of bare limbs emerging from an ultrafeminine frock. Let's not forget arms are one of the most potent and easily stimulated erogenous zones—the soft inside of them is particularly sensitive. Ahem. They're at their best, perhaps, when toned and tanned, so keep a few tricks up your sleeve for enhancing arms even when they're not. If going sleeveless at night or in warmer climes, a deep V or sweetheart neckline that reveals considerable cleavage will inevitably create a happy distraction. As will fabrics that are quintessential limelight stealers: sequins, metallic Lurex, and gemstone-studded silks. Even if you don't know your *Carmen* from your *Tosca* you can still play the diva in above-the-elbow opera gloves: so sleek! Think big, wide, and worldly when it comes to sleeves: the traditional kimono and kaftan and even the dolman with its underarm that extends practically to the waist, offer exotic flair with room to grow!

STYLE ARSENAL GLOSSARY

1. BOLERO:
When a jacket is too much, a tiny bolero is all the sleeve you need.

2. KAFTAN:
Your arms can lose themselves in this Liz Taylor go-to: perfect for parties.

3. DOLMAN SLEEVE:
Go big or go home in a shimmery bow blouse with superloose-cut arms.

4. FLUTTER SLEEVE:
Übergirly, it falls in delicate folds over forearms.

STREET STYLE: GOOD FLEX

Don't have to twist their arms to get big-city babes to sport statement sleeves—the better to hail a taxi with, my dear. From Baroque princess-worthy puff sleeves to overalls with oversize armholes, these exuberant looks show upper appendages in a bold new light. Arms appear strong & dramatic yet every-day: you dress them up *and* take them out.

Not your Disney princess puff sleeves, balloon-size from shoulder to elbow is one way to go for Baroque.

Overalls go urban
We're all over oversize arm-holes as they make any arm look skinny. Edge up this country-boy look with dark glasses and contrasting socks and shoes.

We can see through you
Next best thing to being bare: a transparent three-quarter sleeve.

Safari so good
The secret's in the stretch in a leopard jersey dress.

Swinging
In this whimsical printed swing coat—how fun are pink flamingos?—dark colors act as shading that contour upper arms.

Brush hour
Master the art of the delicate balance with a long shirt sleeve top and a very short skirt.

GET THE LOOK

Dressing ample arms is all about redirecting the eye—and you're the director. Use drama to spotlight neckline, shoulders, and forearms and your upper arms won't be an issue. Oversize short sleeves in pop art colors, maximally embellished collars, shoulders with striking, architectural cutouts. Theatrics helps! Take a good look at yourself in the dress and see how you look head to toe: If your sleeve hits at the heaviest part of your arm, that's where everyone will look. Cropped at the thinnest part of your arm, you're golden. That's why three-quarter sleeves look good on everybody. Long fluted or billowy sleeves—like flared jeans that balance big hips—go a long way toward balancing your upper arms. Any kind of imaginative and fun cuff will create excitement at the wrist and draw the eye away from any I'd-rather-not spots. There's been a strong current of sheer fabrics on the runway the last few seasons, so work this alluring trend to your advantage. Subtle patches of nakedness turn sleeves into eye-catching accessories. And for this reason, when rocking the see-through trend, keep jewelry to a minimum so as not to overwhelm your look.

Okay, so you're wearing your personality on your sleeves with expressive tops, what about the rest of you? Don't go all timid with your bottom half. Rock a skirt that will balance out the razzle dazzle above: swingy pleats, a color-blocked palette, a jewel-encrusted hem, a gorgeous mosaic—anything but basic! A cheerful embrace of ultramodern extras, like crayon colored bangles, mirror sunglasses, quirky color-happy booties, also go a long way toward bringing your arms into balance and refreshing and refining your total look.

Art direction
Dazzling pop art print on drop-shoulder kimono sleeve top pairs perfectly with offbeat pleats.

Hide 'n' chic
So not your boyfriend's sweatshirt: patches of transparency totally transform a sporty look.

Beautiful mosaic
Glimpses of skin through a marvelous mashup of images up the sexy quotient.

Kindest cuts
Befriend a floral-print sundress with sleeves cut out in all the leanest places.

JENNIFER HUDSON

She's Hollywood's flesh-and-blood Transformer, morphing from *Idol* sensation to Oscar-winning actress to red carpet darling. All this, and yet at one point her astonishing talent was nearly eclipsed by a celebrated weight loss of eighty pounds. "I was no longer just 'the voice'!" she gushed to Oprah. "Get my J. Hud on" became a rallying cry for countless Hudson disciples. Having worked hard for her new body, Hudson has since taken fashion fittings seriously. She's learned what best suits her and showcases her shoulder-press toned arms. Two perfect-pitch choices were a sparkling blue metallic Cavalli gown with long lacy sleeves and high slit skirt for 2013 Oscars, and the abstract color-blocked bandage dress by Christopher Kane she wore to a pre-Grammy party in 2014. The off-the-shoulder cap sleeves complemented her bronzy upper arms with a vibrant slash of color. Hudson knows that cleavage and sleek arms work in tandem and uses décolleté-enhancing drapey sleeveless frocks and low-cut sweetheart necklines under blazers to create symmetry—and confirm that her curvy figure's a force to be reckoned with. Her flair for silhouette slimming one-colored suits and column dresses bring a certain song lyric to mind: "One singular sensation . . ."

LOOKS J. HUD'S NOT LIVIN' WITHOUT

Hudson hits the high notes consistently, relying on her standby style solutions.

1.
Her red carpet faves tend toward translucent luxury fabrics like metallic lace and organza that reveal skin in a tasteful, never tacky, way.

2.
She's got it, she flaunts it: J. Hud has a way of working cleavage and tight bright colored miniskirts to her advantage.

3.
Never shy about taking a spin on the color wheel: Hudson plays with a full spectrum of neons, primaries, and metallics.

Mrs. Herrera in her signature white shirt and bolero cardigan. Her model's blazer sports shoulder pads, which can draw attention away from the upper arms.

Ask Carolina

(Mrs. Herrera's designs are well armed.)

What does American fashion's sophisticated lady—who's dressed everyone from Jackie O to Tina Fey—think is every woman's must-have accessory? "A full-length mirror."

Trifecta of arm-slimmers
Julia Restoin Roitfeld in an unbuttoned shirt rolled to three-quarter; Ali Larter's short cuffed sleeve on a floral cocktail frock; organza overlay on a deep V gown cast arms in a flattering light.

You've been a fashion-world supremo for over three decades, yet confess to the occasional style crisis. If there's one go-to piece that can rescue anyone on any occasion, what is it?

CH: For me, a long-sleeved white shirt will always make a woman look seductive and snappy. The beauty of it is there are an infinite number of styles, cuts, and sleeve shapes so every figure can find one. It's a blank canvas that you can dress up or down to capture the spirit of the occasion.

How important is structure and proportion to the success of a look?

CH: Beautiful shapes actually do appeal to the intellect. The eye finds symmetry pleasing. That's why proportion is key. It's not just the design of the dress, but how a sleeve fits the arm, a skirt sits on the hips, when it's on. And there's nothing sexy about a curvy girl in a great dress that's four sizes too small. Style isn't what you wear, it's what you project. If you're comfortable that something looks great on you; you're going to move and act with confidence.

You once said that attention to detail is of the utmost importance in flattering clothes. By that do you mean buttons and zippers and other embellishments?

CH: Actually I prefer clothes that are simple and well made, with maybe one major extravagance—like an organza overlay on a silk gown. The trick is often in the fabric—how it takes shape on your body and stretches with you. What might work for a long sleeve in one fabric might not work for another fabric. Sometimes I'll be designing a dress and decide to take off a sleeve.

One-sleeve sounds sexy, but you've also sent many full-sleeved gowns down the runway—a glamorous godsend for women with not-so-skinny arms.

CH: I've always created clothes that are seductive and sensual, not sexy. I love mystery and there is nothing more seductive than a woman who leaves something to the imagination.

Dressing to Flatter

ABS

Trust your gut to tummy-taming fabrics, high-waist cuts, and color blocking.

Midsection-slimming styles from top: Jane Birkin in highwaist jeans; Sarah Jessica Parker rules in a goddess gown; Kate Hudson rocks a cutout.

ALL ABOUT ABS

Judging from the flowing column-shaped robes of Ancient Greek statues, it's a good bet even goddesses had muffin tops. A slender waist, like a big bust and hips, is a universal sign of feminine beauty, health, and fertility. Achieving the illusion of a slim middle is super easy to pull off—that is, compared with whalebone corsets and gut-busting girdles of great-grandma's day. In addition to an arsenal of shapewear options (more on that in our Lingerie chapter) and straight up-and-down goddess gowns, time-tested tricks include high-waist skirts and pants, drop-waist dresses or no-waist shifts.

One of the great paradoxes about abs is that exposing the top of them, the leanest part, is the best way to flatten and flatter the lower, fleshiest part. The eye is immediately drawn to bare skin in crop tops and cutout dresses. The prehistoric two-piece Raquel Welch wore in the cult classic *One Million Years B.C.* may not be authentically ancient but audiences went wild for the hip-hugging ruffled animal skin sash, and a star was born. Tap into the power of the classic portfolio of get-slim-quick tricks: deftly placed vertical stripes and dark-toned prints, dazzling fabrics, and strategic draping of fabric around the abdomen—all which create the illusion of a midsection so lean it looks like you've spent hours planking, side-crunching, and Zumba-ing.

Curvy cave-babe
Raquel Welch
is in a wrapped
animal hide bikini
in *One Million
Years B.C.*

CINCHED DEAL
A contrast belt draws attention to a higher, natural waistline, skimming lower abs.

Top o' the crops
Offering just a glimpse of flesh, the new crop tops and button-downs-left-undone pair best with high-waist skirts; Naomi Watts flashes more than a smile in a cutout frock. Beyoncé hits the beach in a low-waisted wrap.

1

2

3

Ab-solute truth
1. Paper-bag waist
2. Peasant top
3. Stretch pencil skirt
4. Drop-waist frock
5. Wrapped jacket
6. Tunic top
7. Graphic wrap dress

allocate your
Assets

Who's up for a hundred sit-ups? Didn't think so. Instead, try the sartorial equivalent: dresses, tops, and bottoms designed to slim the middle while boosting your other assets. It's reconfiguring your silhouette by rearranging a few key elements—like dropping the waist from midsection to below the hips or raising the waistline of your pants to a few inches below your bust. Insta-wow!

7

4

6

5

DRESSES

In the days when aristocratic ladies had fashions made for them, they counted on their couturiers to be masters of disguise: dresses would not only be captivating but would deftly dispense with figure flaws. In the tummy-taming department, give props to the empire, the Jane Austen–inspired dress whose fitted bodice ends right under the bust and then flows long and loose over the abdomen. Modern modesty! Other timeless belly camouflage techniques include draping—see the heroic wrap dress—and dropped-waist flapper frocks, both of which hide love handles in plain sight. Elastic body-con dresses seem to carve out womanly curves even hanging on a hanger. Similarly, frocks with strategic splashes of prints disguise bulges and bloat in an oh-so artsy way.

TOUCH OF SASH
Jersey wrap with a gentle drape waist and side sash: the classic route to subtle curves.

BODICE BUILDER
A snug-fit top that skips over abs? Überflattering.

WITH THE BAND
Riffing off shapewear with control fabrics, a bandage-style LBD hugs in all the right places.

Say it with florals
A deep V and high-waist keeps the focus of this cocktail frock all up top.

1

2

Just mad for a mod white leather shift
Waist not, want not!

4

3

SKINNY SPEAK GLOSSARY

1. COLOR-BLOCK TOP: Black stripes down the side of this top tricks the eye into seeing a slim torso.

2. KNOT DRESS: Banish the bloat with a knot-waist that adds interest at the middle.

3. BODICE-FITTING TOP: With accent on the bustline, the waistline is deftly diminished.

4. MIDRISE JEANS: The more moderate version of high-waists can still thwart belly spillover. Make sure it's not a squeeze fit.

PANTS

Thanks in no small part to women designers who tend to be their own muse, trousers are of paramount importance in a daily wardrobe. They're practical and easy to wear and available in an infinite variety of silhouettes. Rejoice in technology's role in how they now fit with the ubiquity of belly-slimming fabrics like spandex and elastane. Pants that hit high above or sit comfortably on your hips are more to your advantage than those that hit you midtummy roll. Lure eyes away from your middle with striking fabrics like glossy velvet and graphic checks. And always think jeans with benefits: besides those with built-in shapewear, there are stretchy high-waist bands and body-grazing boyfriends. Match jackets and pants or revisit your tomboy overalls: the unbroken line of color lengthens torso to no end.

Left: Skinnies seems stingy next to generous-cut high waists.
Below: The legendary Twiggy in a classic torso-extending trouser suit.

BAG IT
Belt a paper-bag waist at your thinnest part; pant legs should flow straight— neither baggy nor skinny.

HIGH THERE
Besides legs looking longer, there's no bulge factor with high waists.

OVERALL IN
Doesn't get more "high"-waisted than this. Add killer shoes and statement jewelry.

SHINY LINE
Sharpen a tight pencil with Lurex sheen— and a flowy top.

A-LINE UP
A+ for school- girl pleats with a high waist.

GET FLAPPY
Geometric interplays of folds, flaps, and slits add visual sharpness.

SKIRTS

Firmly on the fashion agenda each season: flirty skirts of all shapes. From skinny to full, wrapped and ruffled. And there's no reason having a muffin top should rule out any style. A-lines with high waistbands ebb at upper abs and flow at the hips while vertical pleat versions can give the illusion of a flat stomach. Pair pencils with billowy tops in silks and satin that sensuously slide over the body. Wrap skirts should tie midwaist and on the side with a loose top tucked in. As a rule, if there are ruffles or peplums or sashes at the waist, keep tops simple. Or better yet, cropped: a flash of skin here and there sexes up any skirt.

The tummy is tucked away under a full flare, left, and an A-line paired with a top that flaunts those "external obliques."

HOT, HOT, HOT
SWIMWEAR MEETS SLIM WEAR

Your personal best swimwear is a shortcut to bodaciousness and bitchin' hot confidence. Since luxuriating in the sun is all about baring skin, your mission is twofold: keeping your tummy under control while flaunting as much else as possible. Catch the wave of ab-friendly tanks, two-pieces, and cover-ups that showcase only your best assets. Ask any pin up!

1

Maillot my
Play up bust with cleavage, play down belly with dark print.

2

Belly high
A belted high-cut bottom is a waistline's best friend.

3

Corset style
A vertically laced bodice and busy print are like camouflage for your middle.

4

Tankini
All the benefits of a bikini plus complete coverage of the tummy zone.

SARONG TURN
Sofía Vergara's see-through sarong keeps all eyes up top— blame her?

Girl's best friend
Swimming was prohibited in Marilyn's diamond-embellished corset suit.

6

Fly right
Whimsical tropical print and halter straps steal attention from the waist.

5

Scuba do
Sun protection, body slimming, and après-beach-friendly: What's not to like about a scuba top?

KOOL KAFTAN
J. Lo's sheer safari-chic kaftan redefines reveal and conceal.

GET THE LOOK

Potently individual without being navel-gazing: these girls of summer get playful with easy, ab-friendly pieces. From racy crop tops to frilly peplums to floaty smocks, they're meeting high fashion in the middle.

Layer's club A sweet addition to midriff-chic: a pastel layer that flows over abs.

Drop dead glamorous
Dropped-waist flapper dress with sheer panels below the hips steals the spotlight.

Empire striking
Plunge-neck empire mini with sharp peplum pleats strategically diverts eyes from any belly roll.

Arty girl
Genius folds and swathes of sheer fabric form a sartorial take on abstract art while creating the illusion of a skinny midsection.

STREET STYLE: BELLYING UP

No surprise that girls get playful when dressing their rib section— that's where they're most ticklish.

Cozy knit crop top
Redefining transition piece: a midriff sweater! Complete the look with a high-waist pleat skirt.

Mad for plaid boyfriend cardi
Comfortable, cutting edge and cut long enough to top a drop-waist flare skirt. Girl up this collegiate look with a clutch and strappy sandals.

Flare game

The trick to flattering abs here is a peplum that juts out above, not from the waist.

Jumpsuit street

Infinitely flattering: a silky jumpsuit with stripes from the shoulder to the ground.

Get shorty

Belly button baring is so yesterday. Better just a slice of rib cage atop a high-waisted brightly colored skirt. A leather biker jacket takes this look for a wild ride.

Get out the float

A white lacy tent dress publicizes your girly edge while girding your belly size in secrecy.

Posh and pregnant
Victoria Beckham's LBD with a flattering knotted drape waist; the Duchess of Cambridge's same-color scheme creates a streamlined look.

BABY MAMA, IT'S YOU

Think A-listers feel pressure perfecting red carpet looks? Imagine when they're pregnant. How fast baby weight is gained and lost has become a favorite spectator sport. Still, having a child also humanizes stars and there is a lot to learn from their style both when they're sporting a belly or trying, postbaby, to work a recalcitrant bulge back into sexy proportion.

"Bump without the frump" was Ivanka Trump's style goal and her solution was the loose-fit, ladylike empire silhouette. For work, Trump shunned typical maternity wear for tailored below-the-hip blazers and pencil skirts. Out on royal visits, the Duchess of Cambridge's variation on this theme: matching pastel body-skimming shift and fitted top coat; she then extends the blush theme with nude tights and shoes.

"Go long" is the maternity-chic mantra when it comes to accessories: Scarlett Johansson's dangling earrings, Beyoncé's gleaming charm pendant, and even Kerry Washington's cascading side braid cleverly affect an eye-catching vertical line that snatch a little attention from the belly and create a sleek vertical line.

Mother mode
Scarlett Johansson's lacy lowcut; Kerry Washington's empire; Ivanka Trump's scoop-neck minidress; Beyoncé's shape-shifting poet blouse and leggings

How fitting
Ballet-trained
Lubov Azria
lives and
breathes
body shaping:
"If we can't
wear it,
we don't
make it."

Ask Lubov

(Making a case for body con.)

Let the rest of the runway veer toward volume, Hervé Léger's Lubov Azria sits tight with bandage dressing.

If a woman doesn't have a defined waist or even close-to-flat abs, can a dress be the solution?

LA: If the technology is right, a dress or skirt can reshape anyone's figure. Our signature is the individually knitted bandages plaited with high-power spandex. Because of the horizontal wrapping, the body is compressed, resulting in a slimmer, better contoured torso and hip.

You recently said "If we can't wear it, we don't make it." As a former ballerina you not only have an enviably athletic body, but are someone who appreciates comfort fabrics you can really move in. How does this motto drive what you do at Hervé Léger?

LA: During my training with the Bolshoi Ballet I learned a lot about proportion and fit from costumes. Each style is designed to enhance and literally elevate one's look. Today we have spandex that clings, contours, and moves with you. The goal of what I design is to deliver on that experience.

You maintain you're a details person. What role do you assign to patterns and minutiae like zippers, buckles, and buttons in ensuring a dress is flattering?

LA: Seeing is believing: vertically inserted bandages placed around the waist give the illusion of corsetry, helping to sculpt and slim the waist. I love zippers and buckles: they can be inserted at various angles to visually nip the middle and create a slimmer you.

Dress to compress. Three variations on Hervé Léger's abs-molding bandage dress: long and pleated; color-blocked on Nicki Minaj; off-the-shoulder on Doutzen Kroes.

Dressing to Flatter
HIPS

*Bet your bottom: between superflared skirts and low-rise
flowing pants, a whole lotta shakin's going on.*

HIPS DON'T LIE

Booty. No surprise our slang word is the same one pirates use for treasure: Female hips and bottoms are the numero uno erogenous zone, highly prized in every era. When you consider the butt-enhancing bustles of the Victorian age—with hoops, wires, and crinolines being the sartorial equivalent of twerking—you wonder why that era is considered stuffy. Today's equivalent? Those pelvic-bone-exposing low-rider jeans accessorized with candy-colored G-strings. But between bustles—which designers regularly revisit—and baring all lies a happy medium. Fifties icon Brigitte Bardot rocked the now-classic full-skirt sundresses while Shakira actually works her hips into her act. She takes traditional belly-dancer pants and pumps up the volume with feathers, fringe, and chains. A self-styled legend of another era, Marlene Dietrich, who was costumed in body-skimming satin gowns in countless films, chose, in her offscreen life, crisp white shirts tucked into man-tailored pants that she belted to create a sensuous contour. "Darling, the legs aren't so beautiful," she once confessed: "I just know what to do with them." Hollywood's first androgynous icon never traded comfort for cool—or her chorus line–honed figure.

Bustle in flow
Marlene Dietrich's beloved loose trousers; Kerry Washington is in a Michael Kors bustle skirt; Shakira is bellying up; Eva Mendes cinches a goddess gown.

Siren at full sail
Brigitte Bardot made fit and flare world famous.

Got hips?
1. Boy jeans
2. Pleated skirt
3. Peplum top
4. Sheath dress over leggings
5. Boxy car coat
6. Short culottes
7. Fit-and-flare dress

← *GATHER ROUND*
No need to shy away from white: find a skirt with eye-catching folds and slits.

Hips play hide and chic. Clockwise from above: Jason Wu's candy-colored tiered flounces; Emma Roberts in a poufy pin-wrap skirt; powder-blue paper bag waist; Janelle Monáe rocks black palazzo pants.

1

2

3

4

allocate your
Assets

Fashion is ever in a state of flux—lean and minimal one minute, billowy and embellished the next—but womanly hips are forever. Whether you tailor trends to your body or skip them altogether, your goal is always total body balance. Even if (Eureka!) you've found the Perfect Jeans, you're not done till you pair them with the right top. Ideally, one that directs gaze away from the pelvis with bright colors, peplum flares, paper-bag-style waist, or below-the-knee boxy fits.

7

6

5

OP ART
Dark stripes at the edges of the sleeves and dress make the figure appear thinner.

DOLL UP
The ingénue-style sleeveless day dress skips over hips.

GET YOUR FLOW ON

Dresses are the modern, slip-on-and-go option, easing you from boardroom to wine bar with a simple but bold swap-out of accessories. When choosing a silhouette, look to balance the hips and bum with what's on top—with prominent shoulders or sleeves—or below, with the flare of the skirt. Dresses with structured or padded shoulders or puffed or full sleeves distract focus from the hips. Empire waist frocks that cinch below the bust and flow freely over your bottom, create an elegant goddess look for date nights or a Jane Austen book club. For hanging really loose on weekends, tunic frocks and soft-fabric boho chic maxis flatter all figure types. But caution: "flowing" doesn't mean hiding yourself in a tent: if the skirt conceals your hips, bare your legs, arms, or shoulders.

NIFTY FIFTIES
Contrast collar on fit-and-flare frock draws the eye above and below, playing down the hips.

EMPRESS-IVE
Doesn't get more classic or hip-friendly, than a light gossamer, pleated, empire-waist, goddess gown.

WIGGLE ROOM

Curvy girls approach pants shopping like a geometry test: so many sizes and shapes and so little time to make it all fit. The key to the most flattering looks is: keep it simple. Dark or rich-colored flat-front trousers with wide legs that sit a little low on the waist are your go-to. Pants with too high a waist, besides restricting your choice of blouse, will accentuate the waist-to-butt divide. Ditto pleated front styles that create pelvic volume you don't want. And deep-six all side and back pockets as these will visually expand the hips and rear. As for jeans, whether you're a cowgirl or a biker chick, the boot cut is your bestie. The flare of the leg nicely balances the "swell" of your derriere. Pants with elastic waists and/or cuffs—the myriad variations on sweatpants— are the effortless choice as they follow your form without suffocating it.

Left: Hips look sleek in generous-cut pants. **Below:** A sleek leather peplum echoed by flare of pants keeps hips in check.

OL' SPORT
The drawstring waist of athletic-style sweats expand to fit.

↓

SEAMS OK
A dark stripe down the outside of these trousers skinnifies the look of the leg.

↓

↑

LEAN'S IN
Buy trousers one size bigger and have a tailor cut them to fit your body.

MAKE A SWISH
A delicate print, a neutral color, and a ladylike flare at the hem draws eyes down away from the hips.

PRETTY PLEATS
Streamline your shape with sharp vertical folds.

PENCIL CASE
Working-girl staple in a girly print is best paired with a solid man-tailored shirt.

SKIRT CHASE

Two routes to ravishing skirts: reveal and conceal. In the former camp, the pencil, which should hug the body, but not squeeze. For work, pair pencils with a billowy blouse or long, fitted blazer and, for play, a man-tailored shirt that's tunic-length and belted. Nothing conceals so precociously as a pouf and the puffed-out '50s- and '60s-style flared skirt has been unstoppable since the first season of *Mad Men*—in every length from midknee to midcalf. Opposites attract, so if your skirt is voluminous, go lean on top with a tight, stretchy T-shirt or short-sleeved shirt. Another classic skirt trick that's enjoying a comeback: pleats! They're ideal for the modern female who likes freedom of movement. Plus, the vertical folds make your body look longer and leaner.

There's no bulge around the hips or butt that can't be hidden beneath a supersized pouf skirt.

DRIVE, SHE SAID
Pale pink car coat rides easy over slim pants.

SKIN DEEP
Full-length lapels of a python tux draw a slimming line from the collar to the top of the thigh.

AT EASE
Try a graphic print coat casually left open over a cinched skirt.

RUFFLE ALONG
By exaggerating the hip line, riotous pleated ruffles also conceals them.

OUTERWEAR

"The building block from which your whole look is crafted," is how *Marie Claire* creative director Nina Garcia regards the coat. Whether you lean toward classic or cutting edge, there's no shortage of great options with striking cuts tailor-made for your body: from belted wraps and fitted equestrian styles to sweeping cocoons and mod car coats. The optimal strategy for cloaking an ample-hipped figure is to visually create a riot above and below. With color, clever cuts, and killer shoes!

Out of the boxy
Make boxy coats sexy by pairing with skinny pants, or lots of bare leg, or belting in a soft sash.

Clockwise from left to right: Chloë Sevigny's fresh take on an LBD keeps focus on abs and off hips; Adele blossoms in a curve-enhancing cocktail frock.

VANITY FLARE

There's as much art as technology to the most successful red carpet looks. Stylists to the stars must be master engineers who know how well a dress will "hold up" under the pressures of a long night in the full glare of publicity, with paparazzi shooting from every angle. When it comes to managing curvy hips and butt, no expense is spared. They turn to top designers with a genius for figure-enhancing cuts and luxe fabrics that flatter even if they do cost a small fortune. Underneath the glam is a game plan. Whether you're born with one or not, the classic Hollywood starlet hourglass is still the standard shape—and easily constructed. A great number of party dresses play up a slender waist with a softly fitted bodice, fabric embellishments like bows or sashes, and occasionally—for those who dare—a bare midriff. An A-line with a tapered (but not skin-tight) bodice and flared bottom will always slim the shape but not conceal the feminine form. That so many fancy dresses are strapless is no accident: Bare shoulders beg for attention—leaving hips elegantly understated. Juxtaposing a simple, solid color bodice with a froufrou skirt—one with either bold sashes, mermaid flounces, or embellished trim—means the eye will travel well below the waist where you want it. Of course, sleeves and necklines sometimes play scene-stealer. Cleavage will unfailingly call attention to breasts and décolleté, while romantic sleeves broaden the torso and balance your whole silhouette.

Working the va va voom
Sandra Bullock and Catherine Zeta-Jones in satin; Solange Knowles rocks a peplum; Caitlin Fitzgerald strikes a pose in a high-low hem.

87

Carey Mulligan full-metal fit and flare.

Jessica Alba goes for gold in slimming pleats.

Jessica Biel reveals shoulders and legs while discreetly concealing hips.

Beyoncé's strategically placed lace minimizes hips and maximizes arms and thighs.

Left to right: Julie Newmar as Catwoman; Elizabeth Taylor as Cleopatra; Jessica Alba as Nancy in *Sin City*; Kate Winslet as Rose in *Titanic*.

1

2

3

4

DANGEROUS CURVES

The history of Hollywood, like the history of art, is populated with fertility goddesses: big-hipped beauties worshipped for their sexual charms and supremacy. From the mythical Venus and legendary Cleopatra to comic vixens Catwoman and *Sin City*'s Nancy, the woman's power of persuasion was inseparable from her seductress attributes. And her couture was calculated: a tiny waist bookended by boobs and hips of equal proportion. Skinnies, leather pants, and low-riders can always up the rebel ante with belts—worn seductively low-slung, they put hips center stage. Meanwhile, curve-hugging dresses are given a "lift" by low-cut necklines, which offer an expanse of bare flesh and skinny-fit bodices that draw the eye upward. No boxy or shapeless frocks here: power dressing is precision engineered to handle curves!

STYLE ARSENAL GLOSSARY

1. PEPLUM:
Flare or ruffle at waistline of dress or top that juts out over the hips of a woman's bust.

2. A-LINE:
A-shaped dress or skirt, lean on top, flaring at the knee, that conceals the hips.

3. EMPIRE:
Dress or top with waistline that falls just below breasts that draws the eye up away from the hips.

4. PLEATS:
Sharp vertical folds of fabric that seem to lengthen the body.

GET THE LOOK

You're a style junkie with an endless supply of sporty jumpsuits, boyfriend sweaters, romantic frocks and executive chic suits. "Endless" can get you into trouble. How often do you revamp your wardrobe essentials and pare them down so everything is flattering to your nether regions? An occasional clean sweep will clarify what you can't live without and what you can. Learn to look at the big picture of your closet and scrutinize each element: Does this always work for me? Do I feel self-conscious wearing it? Does this top or skirt or pair of sandals always, sometimes, or never pull my look together? A pair of knee-high boots can, for example, balance a short fit-and-flare coat, where a spindly pair of stiletto booties with this topper would make you look top heavy. An oversize belt with a huge buckle is the way to minimize an ample bottom, whereas a sweet skinny belt would emphasize your size. Fabrics are a factor, too: If yours is a closet full of skintight and clingy clothes, swap them out for loose, flowing, or gently fitted pieces. There should be nothing too constricted that butt flaps or muffin tops pop up, and nothing so stiff you look like a cardboard box. Prints or patterns are never neutral: they either enhance body parts or enlarge them. Dark panels or stripes down the side can visually take inches off your hips, while a splash of tiny prints all over proves size doesn't matter—sassiness does. But with prints, think location, location, location. Consider the wisdom of having a pop-colored cartoon character emblazoned on the butt of your pants. Fashion liberation means not having to follow trends unless they work for you personally.

Cinch your waist
A bold, shiny belt helps skinnify a billowy silk jumpsuit.

Cat power
This flared ocelot-print coat is grounded by knee-high black boots.

Transparent motives
A sheer net top will never go unnoticed, meaning less focus on large hips.

Short cut
Pop star meets sports star with puffy overlay over stretchy bike shorts.

STREET STYLE

Swings so cool and sways so gentle . . . like the girl from Ipanema whose mere walking drives the whole beach wild, these urban women hit all the right style notes to keep their hips in harmony. Whether stepping out in fluttery skirts, sporty shorts, or biker-babe leather, they project a playful attitude toward their curves: their style is sexy on their terms.

Shirt dress with full skirt
A skirt that comes full circle adds a spirited dose of movement and minimizes hip area. Bringing the look to the next level of sophistication: an eye-catching pair of fuchsia stilettos.

Bell bottoms balance biker
A playful pair of printed flare pants strike the perfect balance with a short, padded shoulder moto jacket. Notice the dynamic connection between the black beanie and laced booties: an outfit stabilizer.

Print charming
Go with the flow of a painterly print A-line skirt offset by a man-tailored white shirt and slimming black tights.

Gym dandy baggy shorts
Elastic-waist, wide-leg shorts and bomber accommodate curves.

Color-block
Like Constructivist art, this animated mix of geometric abstractons nudges the gaze to the top, then down to the pointy white pumps.

Cinches the waist
It's the smallest part of your midsection—and diverts attention from the hips.

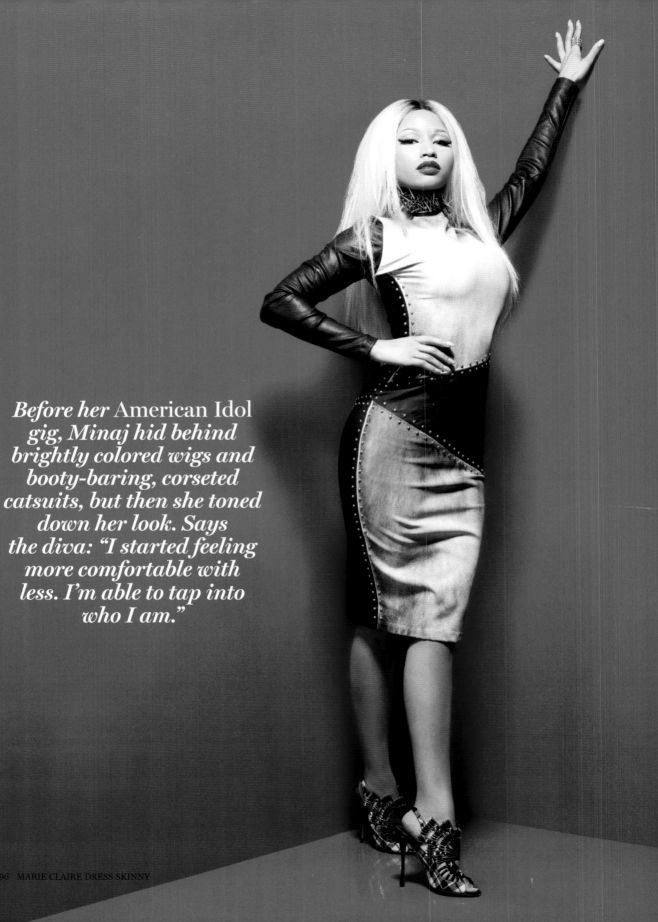

Before her American Idol *gig, Minaj hid behind brightly colored wigs and booty-baring, corseted catsuits, but then she toned down her look. Says the diva: "I started feeling more comfortable with less. I'm able to tap into who I am."*

NICKI MINAJ

A celeb's face used to be her fortune, but these days, when every Disney girl goes badass, it's all about the booty. You gotta shake it to make it. Whether performing or parading the red carpet or city streets, every curvy A-lister learns—generally through trial and error—to manage her assets. "If people are sitting in the barbershop talking about my butt [well] . . . that's what people gonna do," Nicki Minaj once said. And after seeing Nicki in the nude bejeweled body suit at a Hot 97 Radio Thanksgiving concert, well, what else was there to talk about? Minaj has since made style choices that show off her curvyliciousness in a way that doesn't distract from her witty performances and

well-respected rap. She performed at an NBA All-Star game in a pink wig and white bodysuit that was embellished by strategically placed silver ruffles and bustle that equalized her famous butt. She's even taken to wearing beautifully tailored suits—which, of course, she blows out with her signature bubblegum colors. For a recent *Marie Claire* fashion shoot, Nicki zipped into a body-con optical illusion dress where black leather sleeves and side panels functioned like a discreet hip and butt reduction, while the white bodice visually grew her bust. Surely a first: Nicki's top and bottom got equal billing!

NICKI'S STYLE

1.
When it comes to skirts, go va va voom or go home. Skintight, shiny fabrics give her hips a shout out while fit-and-flare princess gowns indulge her royal Barbz persona.

2.
Colorwise, the girl thinks pink. It can be as shocking as her lyrics or girly soft but pink flatters her skin tone and softens her curves.

3.
Bling it on: Nicki favors bold chokers and sparkly necklaces that bring focus up top— a priceless approach to balancing the booty.

97

The designer in his "fresh, glamorous, and graphic" look; a muse in an elegant, gimmick-free bright yellow suit.

Ask Kors

(Michael Kors on style's bottom line.)

The American glamour guru discusses keeping clothes simple (and stretchy) and having your tailor on speed dial.

"THE MORE I STUDIED DESIGNING," Michael Kors once said, "the more I was convinced that elegance was synonymous with simplicity." This is why, with the fashion icon and *Project Runway* judge, you won't find a lot of gimmicks. Just clean-lined pieces in luxe fabrics like cashmere, camel, satins, leather, and mink. "Avoid gathering and heavy fabrics," he cautions about seeking figure-flattering materials and instead go for something with stretch whenever possible. His own uniform of black jacket, black tee, and black or white jeans, he sums up as "fresh, glamorous, and graphic." He did say simple. But also smart and well-planned. He suggests investing in pivotal pieces that will flatter unfailingly: V-neck tunics, flared pants, billowy skirts, and jaunty stripes—as long as they're skinny. With Kors, there's always the give and take between neat tailoring and fluid femininity that modern women find irresistible. Think Jennifer Lopez on *American Idol* in her shocking pink floor-length slash gown. Minimalism to the max. While Kors's most famous muse is lithe-limbed wasp-waisted Grace Kelly, he counts major curve queens from Halle Berry to Jennifer Hudson as clients. Size should pose no limitations on great style, believes Kors. Well, on second thought, he adds, "I think a lot of women have too many miniskirts in their closet."

What is the biggest problem your ample-hipped clients face in choosing looks? What are the best solutions?
MK: Everyone struggles with finding pieces with the perfect fit. Just remember, don't try to force your body into a silhouette that doesn't work for your body or your lifestyle. A full skirt is almost universally flattering, but avoid too many gimmicky gathers and folds. Keep thinking sleek with a slim sheath and insist on stretch in the fabric.

If a pencil skirt belongs in every woman's wardrobe, what kind of tops do you recommend that's sure to flatter the hourglass figure?
MK: Feather-weight cashmere that fits the body is always a chic choice, but I love the appeal of a classic button-down shirt. A loose T-shirt—in say leather or python—looks great belted. If you have a small waist, show it off.

You once said "People always want to look taller and thinner. No one buys a dress because it makes them feel matronly." How important is it for the average girl to get her favorite thing altered so that it fits her perfectly?
MK: Let's put it this way: your tailor should be your best friend. The greatest luxury is to have clothes that look like they were made for you.

Kors's light touch
A classic billowy shirt dress; Jennifer Lopez splits the dif; Karolina in top-to-toe skinny stripes

Dressing to Flatter LEGS

Step it up. Show legs some love with a piquant blend of sleek pants, peekaboo skirts, and well-placed patterns.

Left: A jeans-clad Jane Fonda in '60s western *Cat Ballou*; **Below:** Scarlett Johansson; Jennifer Aniston; and Blake Lively; undress their legs.

LEGS FOR DAYS

"Do my legs look okay in this?" is a relatively modern fashion query. Not so much as an ankle was on display in polite society until nineteenth-century suffragettes demanded dress reform along with voting rights. An inch or two lopped off floor-grazing skirts enabled them to work safely in factories—as well as ride the just invented bicycle. Even gun-toting cowgirls in the 1910s who rode stallions and roped steer had to wear high boots under their suede-fringed pants so no skin would show. Women out West, of course, were the first to popularize jeans and then, as now, it was about free-spirited style. Not to mention showing off their shapely, athletic legs! Over on the East Coast, flappers ushered in frilly, fringed knee-length frocks during the Jazz Age and, according to Wall Street legend, hemlines have been rising and falling with the stock market ever since. Bare legs as a style statement reached a fever pitch in the '50s with short shorts and '60s with mod miniskirts before swinging to the other extreme with groovy '70s maxis. Today everything goes, giving you the option to choose what suits your body best. Are your thighs a little thick, but you've got shapely calves? There's a knee-length pencil skirt with your name on it. We beg to differ with Azzedine Alaia's dictate "If you have long great legs, show them, if not . . . wear long dresses." That's taking the easy way out. If you learn how to balance your figure, reveal the right stuff, and conceal the rest, there's no reason not to rock shorts or a Jen Aniston–style slash gown.

Small wonder
Audrey Hepburn
tucked into white
high-waisted shorts.

Skort circuit
The no-stress way to dress in shorts: a skort.

Rock chicks
Janelle Monáe strikes a biker-babe pose in leather skinnies; Katy Perry plays the lady in flared midi frock; Georgia Jagger takes flight in luxe boy-cut panties.

The seven
1. Strategic print skirt
2. Slimming pattern long shorts
3. Empire-waist dress
4. Gentle flares
5. Slashed pencil skirt
6. Vertical-striped sheath
7. Long vest over black skinnies

allocate your Assets

Getting legs to look good is child's play: a puzzle where you have to make all the pieces fit. If you want to create a thinner thigh, seek black or navy trousers or culottes. Like blush on your cheeks, dark tones can contour legs as needed. Can't part with skinnies? Find a long jacket or vest to top them. Flowing skirts are the flirty choice, while lean pencils do the job with a slit to allow leg some leeway. Keep legs long and calves under wraps with groovy flares.

OPTICAL
Variations on
knee-length
dresses with
thigh-thinning
prints: left
and far left.

FLOUNCY
Strapless body-con
gown with
flounced hem that
hits midcalf:
racy yet refined.

GRAPHIC
Keeping eyes busy with
a bold floral and bare
arms means less focus
on the legs.

DRESSES

'Tis always the the season for flirty frocks in filmy fabrics. The trick: making sure legs are part of the delicate balance. Wraps, slashes, and full-skirted dresses show just the right amount of skin.

Left to right: Fearless frocks with slits, uneven hems, and sheer overlays.

STAYING ON TRACK

Now that we women wear the pants, literally and figuratively, wear them with confidence no matter your measurements. Always buy a size up so the pant leg skims rather than squeeze thighs (you can always get the waist taken in). Bulge-busting skinnies aren't fooling anyone. Floor-sweeping flares are genius for balancing out the thighs, dark panels on the outside slim your whole leg while superwides leave everything to the imagination.

SKINNY LATTE
Same color top to toe creates a sleek canvas. Even the hipster sash over wide leg trousers repeats the scheme.

TAILORED
Menswear-inspired cropped pants in preppy pastel spells country club—chic.

DARK CONTRAST
Black stripes down the side of any pants skinnifies your shape.

GIRL GONE WIDE
Supersized pants will keep leg size a secret but broadcast your fashion cred.

BELLS
Iconic '60s jeans bring the thighs into balance with flared leg.

RUFFLED
Chock-full of assymetrical folds, a basic skirt suddenly steals the scene.

ENDLESS LINE
Nothing lengthens the leg like a lean same-hue skirt that hits below the bust and falls well below the knee.

FULL BLOOM
Sweet! A vivid floral-print circle skirt is a luscious leg cover-up.

GET UNEVEN
Flash 'em just enough with an assymetrical wrap skirt in neon orange.

GO TO ANY LENGTHS

Compared with the torturous business of pants shopping, skirt hunting is a breeze. Leg-flattering options exist at every length and shape. While knee-length is generally the most work-appropriate, both thigh-flashing minis and floor-length kaftans have become weekend go-tos. Pairing same-color tights or thigh-high boots with skirts creates one long, lean line. Bare as much leg as you dare—and add peep-toes—for the same effect.

Left to right:
Kim Cattrall
in *Sex and
the City*;
Sharon
Stone
in *Basic
Instinct*;
Reese
Witherspoon
in *Legally
Blonde 2*;
Alicia
Silverstone
in *Clueless*.

GETTING A LEG UP

"Nice stems" is how a coed sizes up Cher's legs in *Clueless*, and for sure there were more than enough minis, micro kilts, and sheer frocks putting Alicia Silverstone's legs on display to merit the compliment. (Her sheer kneesocks, while covering up lower legs a tad, provide the classic, posh, preppy kicker.) On-screen and off-, good girls and bad girls who use their brains have also learned to use their legs to their advantage. Where once covering them up in pants was a prerequisite for a professional career, now showing legs off in skirts indicates self-assurance. In recent years, it's increasingly fun to go to extremes when off-duty. Fashion has been having fun repackaging and revisiting sexy retro styles that are giving minis a run for their money. Jumpsuits, the once-utilitarian one-pieces worn by parachutists and aviators are making a daring comeback courtesy of Rihanna and Madonna. Full-figured girls love them as they create one slender line from neck to toe. Maxi skirts, often with a big slit skirt, allow you to control how much to show and how much is left to the imagination. Finally, even *Downton Abbey* style mid-calf skirts can look cutting edge worn with cheeky T-shirts and sexy stilettos. Time for tea-length!

STYLE ARSENAL GLOSSARY

1. CULOTTES: Cuffed cutoffs ending just above the knee are the ideal "shorts" for ample thighs.

2. MAXI: Sexier than ever, the '70s staple returns for romantic weekends.

3. TEA-LENGTH SKIRT: Unlike that other '20s emblem, the flapper frock, this demurely reveals the leg's thinnest part.

4. JUMPSUIT: The unbroken line of the "onesie" for grownups is playfully flattering.

GRIN & BARE IT

Why do we love catching a glimpse of our fave glamazons out and about? Because off camera and the red carpet, their street style is *their* style, without benefit of stylist or designer standing by with a made-to-measure gown. No surprise, most of them keep it simple, short, and sweet. Downtime gives us all an excuse to pare things back—plain white tees, cutoffs, shirt dresses . . . Daisy Dukes! Of course, every diva worth her diamond studs might strap on killer shoes to offset the cuteness of a pair of shorts. As a rule, the shorter the length, the more going on top: a crisp button-down shirt, blazer, or loose-fit sweatshirt. A covered-up upper body will increase your confidence for baring legs. Two final words on why celebs' legs look so long: nude shoes! They magically add inches to glam gams.

Left to right:
Ciara; Jennifer Aniston;
Jennifer Lopez;
Cameron Diaz;
Reese Witherspoon;
Diane Kruger;
and Halle Berry.

GET THE LOOK

Think of your body as a sculpture with your legs as the base, and start dressing from there. The objective is to bring your whole silhouette into proportion, and if your legs are on the heavy side, there's no shortage of chic options for lightening up the look of thighs and calves and achieving balance between top and bottom. As for skirts, well, isn't it ironic? Ankle-length skirts—the symbol of prefeminism oppression—have come roaring back to the runway in very sexy incarnations: columns, maxis, wraps. They are most flattering when they suggest rather than flash some skin. Try a slit up to the hip Angelina-style or with a tight, stretchy hem for an exotic sarong look. Slashes are showing up on midis, too, as a way of concealing and revealing simultaneously. Showing just a sliver of skin is a way to be sexy but subtle. And do indulge in a sexy mini if the spirit moves you. Simply pair with a top and matching color tight (thicker the better) for an illusion of one long line of color and excellent coverage. If you prefer your coverage with a side of cool: thigh-high boots. When rocking any full skirt, equalize it with a lean top or blazer, while below-the-hip tunic tops and tailored jackets provide the volume that offsets a skinny skirt.

Darks and neutral pantsuits have their place—they've been a male businessman tradition for more than a century—but never underestimate the power of a bright palette. When chosen wisely, vivid colors can transform your look and project confidence. Reds, oranges, bright blues, and pinks are engaging colors, impossible to ignore. Hillary Clinton's signature monochromatic pantsuits have become the go-to for a generation of working women for a reason: they are universally flattering to all shape legs—which gives you one less thing to worry about. Top of your agenda, boss lady: a curve-enhancing jacket and slender-cut trouser.

Mini to the max Visually connect a tight-fit top and tights, and legs are instantly elongated.

Tunic at night
Enchanted evening guaranteed with a leg-grazing maxi and bell-shaped tunic.

Slash drive
Control just how much leg you want to bare with a tight, knee-length slit skirt.

Suit up
Power red fitted pantsuit paired with black spikes? "Investment" is written all over it.

STREET STYLE: SLIM LIMBS

Artfully dodging traffic, or stopping to take a selfie, these girls-about-town send a clear message about good-looking legs: "sleek" is defined by style, not size. Whether full-flower in a floaty, romantic-print frock, streamlined in a stretchy athletic-style pencil skirt, or sweet-but-sexy in black city shorts, the legs lead.

Curated mix of prints
The louder and clashier the better, graphics ensure bare, bronzed legs look long and well toned.

Swingy, asymetrical hem
The kinetic energy of a cobalt blue swing skirt with an uneven hem is matched by the liveliness of the printed blouse. Sheer patterned tights proffer barely there coverage.

Indie girl fades to black
Gamine-style, rose print minidress with a twist.

Long sleeves, short shorts
Opposites are attractive when covered arms meet nearly bare legs, courtesy of cuffed shorts.

In line
Jock-inspired, striped jersey pencil and near-matching cropped hoody team up to streamline a sporty silhouette.

Down on your knees?
Never. For many, minis will always be the height of fashion. Balance bare legs with blouson jacket.

Being teased about being chubby as a child made her stronger, Zooey claims. But rather than dress tough, she holds fast to her unfailingly charming style offscreen. Girly's her look and she's sticking with it. Still, she admits: "I don't have control over what's on-screen and that's terrifying."

ZOOEY DESCHANEL

Burning up Hollywood as an award-winning comic actress, accomplished singer, and funky style icon, Zooey Deschanel also trained as a dancer—and has the muscular legs to prove it. Given her multitalents and unique gamine-next-door style, the native California girl seems primed for a long career in the spotlight. What makes her a favorite of fans and paparazzi: her kooky-sexy allure and genuine compassion as a role model. "I always felt like a bit of an outsider, and now I'm an outsider who's a satellite for other outsiders."

Sure she's got a playful approach to fashion choices, but the world takes them pretty seriously. When there's a pink taffeta gown that screams prom queen, she'll add daring décolleté; for a touch of punk she'll pair black leggings with a fuchsia print mini to make her legs long and lean. Having outgrown the cutie-pie stage, we knew she'd be more than up for the challenge of rocking a cropped black blazer with panties look for a *Marie Claire* cover shoot. She aced it by creating one long unbroken line of color: black tights, boots, and black hair bow to tie it all together.

THE *NEW GIRL*'S OLD TRICKS

1. Shorts and tights
The thinking girl's short shorts are paired with leg-slimming dark tights.

2. Girl in full
Zooey thinks big about skirts: A–lines are reliably flattering to waist and thighs.

3. Prom time
Party dressing is a Zooey specialty: curve-enhancing pink satin gowns, sequin sheaths, and prom-inspired pouf skirts.

HIGH LINE
Recipe for slim look: mix black high-waisted pants with supersized chubby fur.

CUT IT OUT
Vibrant pencil and midriff affords a sneak peek at the abs and lean calves.

SHORTS CIRCUIT
Olivia Palermo upgrades sassy print shorts with classic dark blazer from the Milly x Banana Republic collection.

AskMichelle

(The Milly chief's long view of legs.)

You know what they say about French women! Milly's Michelle Smith, who trained in Paris at Dior and Hermès, designs parfaitement *figure-flattering fashion.*

Pants are given prime real estate in every Milly collection. From wide black paper-bag waists to skinny print pantsuits. Is there a pair that truly "looks good on everyone"?

MS: Your go-to pants have to be comfortable on you, otherwise you won't feel or look confident. As a designer, I try every pair on to make sure every detail is perfect. If I had to pick one style that tends to look good on everyone, it would have to be a skinny black pant. It can be teamed with a T-shirt or a chubby fur as long as the silhouette is sexy and feminine. A sheer blouse is good for attracting the eye and alleviating the heaviness of black. The first place I look for inspiration is always fabric and color. It's also fun to punctuate your look with a printed pant every season. A tailored blazer and white shirt over printed shorts is a smart alternative to a miniskirt. Also, matching print tops and bottoms affect one long slender streak.

Below-the-knee skirts have become a fixture again on the runways and certainly a boon to the majority of women who don't like showing too much leg. How important is cut and texture in ensuring a longer skirt assumes a flattering shape and fab, not-frumpy look?

MS: When wearing a longer skirt with lots of fabric and different textures, go simple on top and you'll look much more modern. One of my all-time favorite looks is a very fancy embellished skirt with an easy white tee—the unexpected pair creates an effortless look that's simply fabulous. Bare arms and bare legs will also lighten up the look. Also, if you're afraid you'll look dowdy, slip on a pair of killer heels.

You're a master of the scene-stealing pencil skirt—offering them in everything from electric hues to metallic leathers to contemporary prints. How should a bigger girl approach fabrics and patterns?

MS: Pencils accentuate female curves, making you instantly sexy. I like to put a twist on the tradition with bold prints on modern fabric. Vivid colors with blacks can work together to create flattering contours; and then you want to offset this with a simple tank and heels. Occasionally I like to work in a sliver of skin with a cropped top; it's usually the leanest part of your middle section so why not draw attention to it? I've also been moving toward a relaxed silhouette, pairing lean skirts with sweatshirts. Two timeless players.

Allover prints are seductively slimming with strategically placed dark panels and sheer or cutout features, as in Sarah Harding, formerly of the band Girls Aloud.

Workout wear
WOW!

*Splash out on the new color-drenched, control-fabric activewear
and look super hot while staying fit.*

RUN THE WORLD

From top:
Sporty chic's come a long way, baby. From top: Marilyn Monroe in gym bloomers; Jennifer Aniston in miniboxers; Gwyneth Paltrow in cropped leggings; and Julianne Hough looking fighting-fit in a tie-dyed tee.

Game on, glamour girls! American women who exercise spend no less than 511 hours a year doing it—time we work our workout look, yes? Thanks to the surge in year-round routines like yoga, Pilates, Zumba, and SoulCycle, activewear is now a multibillion dollar business with runway megastars like Stella McCartney, Alexander Wang, and Tory Burch, the latest to bring their A game to performance designs. With adrenaline-pumped alphas spending so much time together in such close proximity, there's greater motivation to look gorgeous when you grunt and sweet when you sweat. Looking fab can be an incentive to just getting started with a new sport. And don't sweat it: the new activewear incorporates fabrics that wick away sweat, tame bulges, and stretch every which way with every type of body. Tory Burch recently hinted at perhaps the biggest reason tanks, leggings, and shorts must go the distance: "A lot of women wear what they wear to the gym all day long."

And stretch
The original "Blondie" (Penny Singleton) from the eponymous '30s films shows her calisthenics moves in basic cottons. Techno-materials like spandex that support boobs and muscles didn't arrive until the '80s.

CELEB STYLE

A-listers prove that killing it on the red carpet starts with making their body the sexiest outfit of all.

Camila Alves heads to a workout in ever-slimming black leggings and color-block jersey.

Liv Tyler's chic body-con monochrome wet suit is like an LBD for the life aquatic.

Facing stiff competition on the red carpet inspires celebs to tone their bodies—and look their best doing it. **From left:** Yoga-bound Emma Roberts in black tights; Rita Ora flaunting abs of steel in neon stripes; Miranda Kerr no doubt looks pretty while planking in cropped leggings.

Actress Vanessa Hudgens layers an oversize skull sweatshirt over leggings and tee. Pink laces tie it all together.

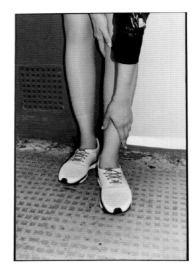

Crunch time
Same rules apply to Stella McCartney's workout wear as everyday wear: legs look best with similar shaded legs and shoes; arms are skinnified by full sleeves; monochrome outfits create a leaner silhouette.

allocate your
Assets

Consign military grays and neutrals to guys and juice up activewear with a mix of color-block neons, flashy prints, and preppy primaries. Celeb trainer Jillian Michaels' motivating motto "Get comfortable with being uncomfortable" might apply to cardio class, but not your clothes! Slip into deliciously soft fleece, nylon, and elastane that holds and molds in the right places.

Workout must-haves
1. Spandex tank
2. Color-block sneakers
3. Relaxed jersey dancer tee
4. Brightly colored sweats
5. Neon stretch jersey
6. Layered mini-boxers
7. Graphic sports bra
8. Patterned stretch hoody

1
2
3
4
5
6
7
8

Mirror, mirror
The *Project Runway* icon limbers up in pieces from her New Balance actionwear collection, HKNB. Says Klum: "During a workout, I won't really get into the zone and keep going unless I'm feeling like a girl! It's why I include so many flirty and feminine floral patterns." The sports bra and sneakers, however, have to be all about support and "performance technology."

ASK HEIDI

Model icon-cum-activewear designer Heidi Klum says
"Auf Weidesehen" to boring, incentive-killing gym clothes:
"I'm trying to bring the runway to the treadmill."

"Strength Is Stunning," "Fierce Meets Fit," "Head-Turning and Heart Pumping," are some catchwords used to describe HKNB, your activewear line for New Balance. What's so sexy about a strong woman?

HK: Often a stronger personality will follow getting fit. I've seen so many people just transformed! A strong-bodied woman follows her dreams and that takes confidence. And confidence is always sexy!

What inspired you to collaborate on an activewear line—why not party dresses?

HK: They don't need me to make cocktail frocks; plenty of brilliant designers out there do that. Instead, I'm trying to bring the runway to the running track and treadmill. Workout gear should not only enhance your workout but make you look great. Great-looking style can be a driving force whether you're hitting the gym or fitting in a quick run or yoga class. My goal is equal parts athletic and aesthetic!

Do you have different styles for different sports—say running vs. Pilates?

HK: If you're on a budget, there are certainly a lot of pieces that work for both indoor and outdoor sports. My signature floral prints are fun for an all-girls Pilates class but sturdy and bright enough so cars can see you if you're running out on a road. Scientists have proved that bright colors not only boost brainpower but lift your mood.

What are the biggest style mistakes women make when it comes to workout wear?

HK: I think when going for a run or bike ride by yourself it's tempting to just throw on a loose shapeless T-shirt or maybe your boyfriend's cutoff sweats. When you go to the gym and everyone sees you, it's a different story. Performance wear you feel good in will make you want to work out more—and then you'll start seeing results. The more your hard work starts to pay off and you love the results, well why not shop for even sexier pieces—printed sports bras or short boxers?

Why include bras and sneakers in your line?

HK: I was only interested in doing an activewear line that was legitimate, where you'd really get in the support you need during any kind of vigorous or high-impact exercise. Needless to say, a supportive bra is essential for any kind of aerobics and only precision-engineered sneakers will reduce the strain of running and sports like tennis.

So much workout wear is "body-con"; is there a reason it's so close-fitting and revealing?

HK: Especially for those activities when you're working with a trainer or instructor, it's helpful for him or her to see the outline of your body to ensure you're keeping the correct form while doing the moves. But it also gives you a chance to see what you look like; if you're working toward changing your shape, you can mark the progress.

ACCESSORIES

Dainty isn't cutting it. Embellish big-time with statement bangles, baubles, bags, shoes, and shades.

ADORN THIS WAY

An accessory, as Webster's defines it, is an accomplice—it helps get the job done. In this case, looking fabulous head to toe. Shoes, boots, bags, bling can breathe boldness into a look—ideally without overpowering it. The dangling gemstone earrings with a body-con LBD, the supersized-cuff with a crisp white shirt, the DayGlo-dyed exotic skinned tote with your fave jeans: it's the conversation starter when you walk into a party. "A statement necklace dares a person not to look at you when you're speaking," says designer Maria Cornejo. "Whether it's dazzling colored diamonds or, as I prefer, something natural like feathers or horsehair, it will not only enhance a dress's neckline, but give the woman attitude." So exploit these little scene-stealers to your advantage. Placing eye-catching sparkle, colors, and ornamental trim in key places will assure that's where you get attention. Say you've snagged an awesome A-line dress that grazes your curves ever so slightly and you've added same color opaque tights so your legs go on forever; now it's time to go in for the killer accessory. Let a silver-tipped stiletto, candy-colored bags, or a knockout necklace create a little epicenter of interest in areas you want to display. Think bold strokes. You're the masterpiece and these are the finishing touches.

Are you ready, boots? Sixties pop star Nancy Sinatra and the white go-gos that cruised to the top of the charts.

Happy Feet
1. Flat strappy sandals
2. Camel raffia wedge
3. Pastel color-block spikes
4. High-heeled d'Orsay
5. Pointy cow-bootie
6. Sheer cut-out sandal
7. Crisscross Maryjane

ARMED FORCES
An embellished stiletto's low vamp (far left) and a d'Orsay's cutout sides flatter legs by extending the amount of bare skin on display.

This is the moment to exercise your groovy '70s muscle with funky suede over-the-knee boots, long fringed python, and skin-toned cork platforms. Skin is in!

OMG Shoes

Sexiest thing on two legs? You in a shoe or boot that's to-die designwise and enhances the look of your foot and leg, too. Generally, the lower the cut of the vamp, pointier the toe, and higher the heel, the longer and leaner your legs will look. Longer still if you match the shoe to your skin tone. Props to the classic nude d'Orsay slingback with cutaway sides: possibly the world's most flattering shoe!

Stripe session
Eye-catching patterns lure the eye to the shoe; the nude color lengthens the calves.

The shining
A gilded, ornamented wedge and (below) a gleaming patent booty become the focal point of your look.

THIGH HIGH THERE
Pairing nude over-the-knees with a mini gives you legs for days.
→

HEEL THYSELF
Open-backed sandals will slim down the ankle.

←

Runaway slide
Cork wedged slides have the substance to balance big calf muscles.

Good grounding
A solid criss-cross wedge will be in proportion to a curvy body.

GRAND OPENING
A lacy-pattern stiletto slide for the ultimate skin exposure.

→

Gladiator glam
A cutout-patterned heeled sandal both reveals and conceals.

Eternity boot
No better way to balance a pear shape than a black leather thigh-high peep-toe.

Cut-out booties
Flashes of ankle (above and left) are a sexy distraction (and can also cover up cankles!)

Très bow!
Expect to have the world at your feet with magnified bow stilettos.

Fierce feet
A contrast leopard-print toe and heel draws the eyes away from the lower legs.

Boots as tights
Balance a full-floral skirt with a pointy suede knee boot.

Full of lace
Fashionista version of contrast laces on sneakers.

Footloose modern
Midi skirts, left and above, showcase calves and calf-slimming heels.

Size matters
A kitten heel might vanish on a large foot; a midheel strikes the right balance.

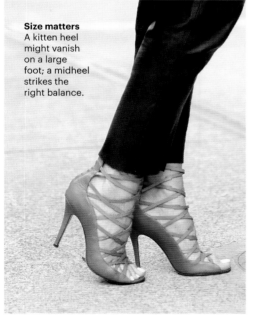

Power platform
Keeping a mega-platform sandal the same color as the skin will give the ankle shape.

Toe the line
Skinnifying
legs starts
and ends
with the toe:
whether
superpointy
or peep-toe.

SOLE SISTERS

A Cinderella moment? Like A-listers headed to a ball, the style-savvy know happy endings hinge on the perfect-fit shoe! Slip on strappy vixen stilettos, peep-toe pumps, and bejeweled sandals with infinite skin on display to ensure you're ready for your close-up.

Steppin' out
Attention-grabbing tactics include contrast toes, like on Rihanna and Katie Holmes, and fanciful metallic embellishments.

FIT Bags

Seriously? A bag that works like a diet? Put it this way: a bigger bag will balance out proportions while a structured one will give a curvy body angles. Too-tiny bags against an ample body can look like a misplaced brooch, especially if the color pops. Size up the situation by noting where the bag falls: If a short-strapped shoulder bag hits right at your upper arms—which you'd rather not shine a light on—wear clothes the same color. But if you want to flaunt those limbs and distract from elsewhere— go with neons, prints, or something embellished.

2 *3* *1* *4* *6* *7* *5*

Hand candy
A striped miniclutch
coordinates with
this outfit.

A BIG LUG
Worn over the
shoulder or
on the crook of
the arm, this
bright bag will
beam light
wherever it falls.
→

Blue not
A chain bag
rectangula
slice of blu
complement
a soft jerse
froc

LOVE HUE
A power red top handle adds textural interest without breaking a long line of color; an emerald green shoulder bag doubles as a precious pendant. →

Fringe fest
Long colorful fringe adds length and drama to your shape.

Skin-telligence
As in nature, a colorful python shoulder bag is camouflaged against cool abstract-print sleeves.

Envelope please
Picking up on the sheen of the top and track pants, an envelope clutch adds a touch of sass.

HELLO BOHO
Sling a hippie-chick icon over your shoulder and wear with the same-color blue dress. →

Cash and carry
An iconic Hermès satchel elevates a funky print.

White on
Minimalist take on layering: white texture bag against white skirt.

Round up
An oval-shaped camel clutch echoes the scoop of the knit vest.

Little black bag
Against a bright coat, Chanel's LBB becomes the pop of color that calls attention to the hip and butt zone.

Trapezy does it
A bright Cèline top-handle satchel stands out against black leggings. Wearing a red skirt or pants would create an unbroken line.

Neon nano
Tiny bags—
a brilliant way
to accent with
a fave color.

Hot spot
A potpourri
of polka
dots pulled
together
by color-
coordinating
clutches.

Label love
Sparkling "star"
rings grab a neutral
Givenchy clutch
by the logo.

Ornamental case
Just what the LBD
needed: a handful
of sparkle.

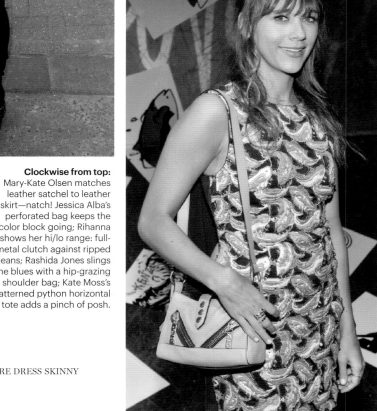

Clockwise from top:
Mary-Kate Olsen matches leather satchel to leather skirt—natch! Jessica Alba's perforated bag keeps the color block going; Rihanna shows her hi/lo range: full-metal clutch against ripped jeans; Rashida Jones slings the blues with a hip-grazing shoulder bag; Kate Moss's patterned python horizontal tote adds a pinch of posh.

TRUE GRIP

If you can carry a movie—or a tune—you carry a showstopping bag: precious gem-encrusted minaudières, minimalist box clutches, exotic skin totes, and icon top handles. Best-dressed-listers know that getting a look together is an ensemble production and the bag does its part to balance things out. A bright clutch you carry at the hips lures all eyes there, while a vivid tote spotlights your thighs. If you're keeping the same color, mix textures: black leather with black fur, blue python with jeans! And why stop there? Coordinate rings and cuffs with your clutch. Bling it on!

Want to distract eyes from hands or arms? Load up on rings, bracelets, and precious clutches.

Bold accents to
shine light on
your assets
1. Abstract
choker
2. Embellished
cuff
3. Vivid stone
ring
4. Dynamic
dangles
5. Red patent
watch
6. Stack of
bangles
7. Priceless
pendant

1

2

3

4

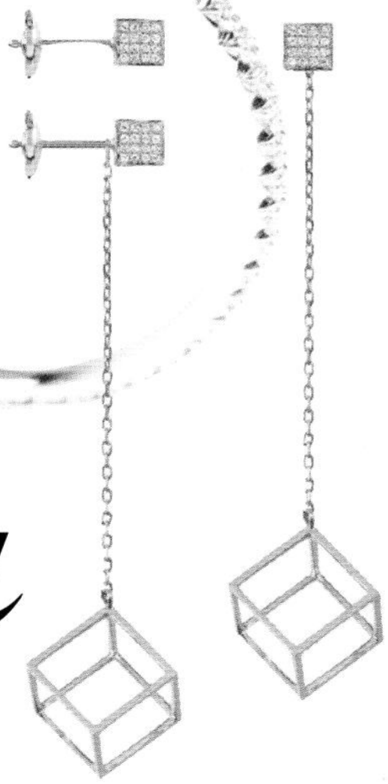

5

XXL Jewels

Go big or go home is the manifesto when you want jewelry to skinnify your face, neck or hands. Shiny statement pieces will attract attention to or away from wherever you please. That doesn't mean bedeck yourself head to toe like a bejeweled Byzantine empress, one or two key pieces will provide all the dazzle you need. Neither does embellishing mean breaking the bank: there's treasure to discover in metals, shells, enamel, and wood—not to mention a huge spectrum of glass beads and gold plate. Get into costume!

7

6

Delicate rings on every finger complement a fine-lined tattoo.

Carey Mulligan's chic in chandeliers that elongate her neck and offset a pixie do.

Angelina Jolie's bright green drops glisten against her golden skin.

Giovanna Battaglia blooms in a floral necklace, hair embellishments, and butterfly earrings.

Amy Adams's gemstone bib draws the eye downward, making her neck appear leaner.

Juxtaposing extremes of black beads on Beyoncé's headdress, earrings, and dress creates a retro-fabulous effect.

The kinetic movements of Blake Lively's dangling ruby drops dazzle the eye—and match the gown!

Whether diamonds or rhinestones, a sparkling bracelet or low-hanging choker is a flattering insta-attention-getter.

BELTS

Whether cinched over a red carpet goddess
gown or casual blouse and pencil, a belt
is like a beacon illuminating and defining
the waist: the epicenter of the female form.
Sure, some days you put together a top, skirt,
and shoes like a crazy quilt, but a belt can
pull it all together. Still, while the right belt
can flatter you, the wrong one's a frenemy.
Position is everything. You need to find your
sweet spot—which may be your natural waist
or right above it (you'll know it when you
find it). If you've got a big tummy, wear the
belt above your waist, while if you're boobs
are most prominent, cinch the belt a little
below. Widthwise, there are hippy '70s belts
worn low-slung and corset-belts that can
cover your entire middle—just make sure
you don't create a bulge. If you're belting a
waistless dress or top, you're better off with
skinny belts, as a wide one will cause fabric
to bunch up. Naturally, color counts, too,
as a contrast belt will call attention to the
waist while a same-color belt and outfit will
provide countouring. And whether dressing
red carpet or super casual, think like a techie:
colorize areas you want to flaunt with brights
and graphics and minimize those you don't.

Holding pattern
Jennifer Lawrence's wild see-through gown was tamed and shaped by a sturdy clasp belt.

Good nudes
Blake Lively's tan belt complements same-color stilettos, effecting symmetrical perfection.

A lot of curve
Hourglass figures like Scarlett Johansson's benefit from shape-making belts—otherwise dresses look boxy.

Cinch mob

With sashes, cinches, wraps, corsets, chains, and belts with big buckles, it's not so much about what to wear as where to wear them: Place belt on the abs, just under the lowest rib to define waist and balance your shape. If you're short-legged, wearing the belt just below the boob will lengthen the look of your legs. Wearing a wide belt below the waist can bring big boobs into balance.

Sunnies side up
1. Big aviators
2. Mirror wayfarer
3. Ladylike cat-eye
4. Metallic cat-eye
5. Colored lens wayfarer
6. Color-block rectangle
7. Patterened wayfarer
8. Retro cat-eye

Shady character
Tori Praver in oversize aviators.

EYE ON Sunglasses

"My sunglasses are like my guitar," Patti Smith once said, and as with the Olsen twins and "Gangnam" guy Psy, shades are so much a part of some celeb identities they wouldn't recognize themselves without them. For sheer style, sun protection or hiding a hangover, they're a year-round must-have, so very worth securing a flattering style for your face. The general rule: round and curvy styles will accentuate fleshy faces, so think angular—squares, rectangles, and linear brow bars. Vintagey cat-eyes with their upsweep at the outer edge elongate and lift the face. And there's no end to the wayfarer variations with their iconic trapezoid frame and sturdy arms.

1

2

3

4

5

6

7

8

SHIELD
Supersized neon-hue shields are best for women with strong features; keep the rest of the look neutral!

Funky vision
Wayout wayfarers are a counterpoint to the edgy, embellished top.

WIDE-EYED
Round glasses offset a square jaw, while a heart-shaped face like Eva Mendes's looks best with shades with a little lift that highlights the cheekbones.

Hello, kitty
Curvy queen Dita Von Teese opts for oval frames that balance her long, lean face.

Scenester
Olsen's square frames equalize her round baby face.

Getting her wayfarer
Straight-framed, structured wayfarers complement Gisele Bündchen's symmetrical face and long flowing hair.

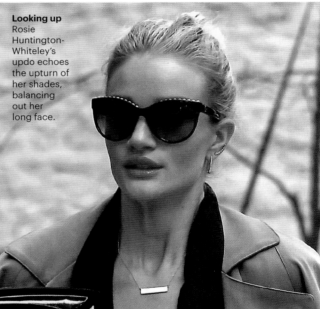

Looking up
Rosie Huntington-Whiteley's updo echoes the upturn of her shades, balancing out her long face.

CLEAR-EYED
Transparent frames are a modern take on iconic wayfarers.

The designer
takes a long
look at his
nautical-
clad model.
A single chain
necklace
repeats
the flattering
scoop of
the neck.

Ask Tommy

(Hilfiger on the extras factor.)

While the iconic designer remixes and remodels American preppy, his accessories provide the spin.

You've always said that your designs reflect your passion for rock and roll. Your pop-inspired preppy clothes are your signature; how does the music reverberate with your shoes and bags?

TH: I was a teenager in the '60s, so was always loving the *Rolling Stones*'s album covers and the really cool clothes and boots they wore. I try to channel a rock attitude through bold, sexy, colorful shoes, funky patterned boots, and edgy, graphic-print bags.

To extend the music metaphor, a handbag at Tommy Hilfiger is never just a backup, it's a headliner in its own right. From vibrant color-block top handles to bright, soft clutches to sporty duffels. If you could choose one that would flatter every figure what would it be?

TH: The general wisdom is that the bigger the body, the bigger the bag but my thinking is: no bag should be off-limits if you love it. You choose the shape and size depending on the occasion and what you're wearing. Each season I like to update classic shapes—clutch, tote, backpack, and duffel—with new colors and fabrics. One season, we did everything in a saturated California surfing palette, because the collection was sun-bleached. So wherever you wore the bag on your body it was tone-coordinated, so it created a nice harmonized silhouette.

A lot of the shoes in your most recent collections are what you'd call hipster/prepster. Punchy primary-colored flat sandals; chunky-heeled two-toned Oxfords and white high-heeled loafers with black knee socks. What's the most flattering shoe out there today?

TH: A classic flat is always an essential. One of my favorites is the sporty flatform sandals, which combine a flat sole and a low platform. It's substantial enough so it will never look spindly no matter the size or shape of one's calf; they're also a great way to lengthen the leg with a bit of height.

Tartan beat A roomy plaid tote picks up where a minikilt ends, extending the line of the leg.

You paired quite a few looks with knee socks. What about this schoolgirl look should grown-up women find appealing?

TH: Knee socks worn with a heeled penny loafer function just like a cool boot. It's a color-block look and classically mod. But anything knee-high looks good on every shape leg and body type. Worn with minis, shorts, or cropped pants, they elongate the legs, making them look leaner.

Plaid handle
Tommy updates traditional tartans with cartoon blue.

Chain spotting
A minimalist translation of multiple ropes? Black on black.

Camel light
Shorten the strap of a suede shoulder bag for an insta-top handle.

Muse-worthy
Zooey Deschanel in a mod-inspired shift from her Tommy capsule collection.

Off the grid
Hailee Steinfeld poshes up a boyish hunting jacket with a girly pleated skirt.

Well-schooled
A plaid and camel suede knapsack's a smart partner for matching booties.

Escape fantasy
A color-block beach-size tote counterbalances bare legs.

Check it
Cheeky kneesocks stand in for boots in an irreverent take on the traditional Brit houndstooth.

Dressing Skinny with LINGERIE

Let's flesh this out: how fabulous clothes look on you depends on perfect-fit underpinnings.

AN INSIDE JOB

The bare facts are these: everyone with a bust and hips is technically "curvy"—from Camilla Belle, who's a size 4, to Christina Hendricks, who's a size 14. No two women's assets are exactly the same shape or size or in the same place, and *vive la différence*. But the takeaway here is that accommodating curves is a completely personalized, your-body-and-yours-alone matter, and it starts with lingerie. Before you splurge for that luxury LBD or executive sheath, invest in a perfect-fit bra and panty. You can't build a killer wardrobe without an unshakeable foundation. The good news: figure-flattering lingerie is no longer the tortuous, faint-inducing business it once was when abdomen-compressing corsets were made of whalebone, metal, and wood. Both luxury and foundation fabrics now let you control and reposition your assets but feel sinfully good and appear so invisible you'll forget you're wearing them. Unless, of course, you don't want anyone to forget you're wearing them. Since a few rebellious designers in the '80s unleashed über-girly underwear as outerwear on the runway, the trend is still going strong. Corsets, bras, and panties worn in public have become symbols of empowerment that are finally giving the female form the exposure it deserves.

Italian actress Sophia Loren, who frequently filmed in lingerie, knew just how much to cover up: "Sex appeal is 50 percent of what you've got and 50 percent of what people think you've got."

Hidden assets
1. Midrise panty
2. Lurex long-line
3. Lace bodysuit
4. Spaghetti-strap bra
5. Pink satin briefs
6. Silk bikini
7. Floral bustier

SLIP SERVICE
A multitasking bra slip makes any frock fit better.

Eternal feminine
From the simplest camisole to a full-length lace slip dress to a black bra top straight out of *Mad Men,* lingerie assumes many guises and suits every shape and size.

1

2

3

allocate your
Assets

7

Since Ancient Roman days, when women wore custom-made leather breast cloths, lingerie has been fashion's supreme multitasker: protecting outer clothes from perspiration, supporting boobs, providing shape, and seducing a lover or attracting a new one. No surprise that all the luxury fabrics, embellishments, and precision technology that go into today's lingerie result in increasingly robust sales, recessions be damned. Sexy always sells.

5

6

4

You raise me up
1. Bustier with built-in bra
2. Classic long form
3. Lacy underwire
4. Push-up
5. Spandex V-neck bra
6. Stretch shapewear

LOVE ON TOP

Whether or not rumors are true that Wonderbra billboards were so erotic they caused car accidents, it's a given: the eponymous push-up bras are all about provocative. More all-purpose options for the big-bosomed include underwires for extra support, long-form for abs control and sports bras for bounce-minimizing. Go for a professional fitting! The perfect-fit bra not only guarantees clothes drape better; they're good for posture. Stand tall!

Boudoir call
Doutzen Kroes
combines a girly cami
with a crisp white
menswear blazer.

Negligee bust-haves
1. Elastic camisole
2. Chiffon chemise
3. Lacy tank
4. Satin slip
5. Shirred bustier
6. Fitted camisole

SWEET NOTHINGS

The deliciously flimsy boudoir classic, the camisole, is a luxury every big-busted babe can slip into as long as there's built-in support, full coverage, and sturdy straps (try before you buy!). Camis can also double as a little bit of louche layering under a sheer bodice blouse; depending on the climate, you may also wear a bra under the cami for extra warmth. What's not to love about the retro term "negligee" for any lace-trimmed sheer silk slip? It's from the French word for neglect— as in she neglected to get fully dressed! The irresistibly termed "teddy" is the boudoir's answer to the bodysuit: a one-piece that covers top and bottom yet leaves little to the imagination.

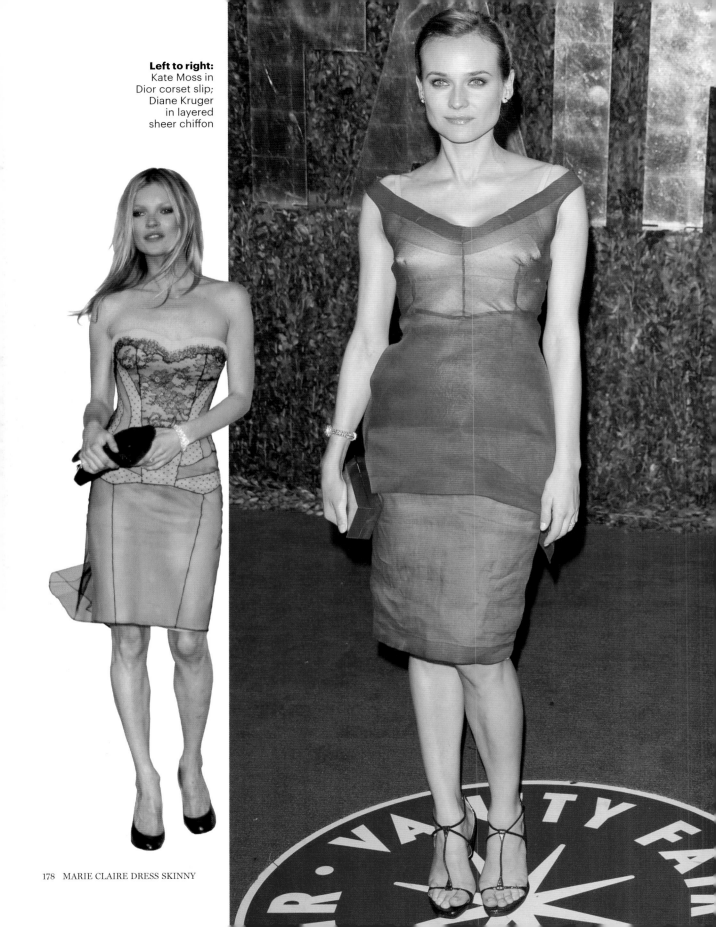

Left to right:
Kate Moss in
Dior corset slip;
Diane Kruger
in layered
sheer chiffon

THE BEST UNDRESSED LIST

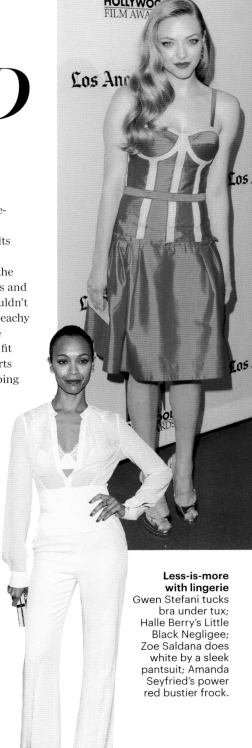

Unlike the rest of us, actresses and models are often paid to take their clothes off, so it's not exactly a shocker many of them slink onto the red carpet in ravishing lingerie-inspired looks. But note first how they haven't worn the trend: There's no costumey corsets with lace bodices and in-your-face cleavage, no garish Can-Can girl garter belts holding up thigh-high stockings. The true style icons keep it simple, minimal, and modern. Kate Moss wore a lace-bodice dress that "suggested" corset but was in fact the simplest strapless sheath. She adds a single diamond cuff and matching black pumps and clutch and *fini*! Gwen Stefani wearing a black bra to the American Music Awards couldn't have looked more elegant tucked under her pearl-embellished black tuxedo jacket. Beachy waves, rather than an overdone do, upped the cool factor. Besides dressing down the luxury lace, chiffon, and satin of lingerie, red carpet royals have learned that perfect fit merits center stage. Boobs don't spill over bodices or pop out of arm holes, sheer skirts stop short of the always-regrettable crotch shots. The social media world may be hoping for a wardrobe malfunction but always best to leave 'em wanting more.

Less-is-more with lingerie
Gwen Stefani tucks bra under tux; Halle Berry's Little Black Negligee; Zoe Saldana does white by a sleek pantsuit; Amanda Seyfried's power red bustier frock.

Dita Von Teese's burlesque-inspired hourglass corset dress.

Julianne Hough in a sheer layered tank and tea-length slit skirt.

Lea Michele in a black, lacy deep V neck slip dress.

Selena Gomez in a navy peekaboo corset gown.

SHEER NERVE

The sexy '60s fashion frenzy wasn't the only symptom of *Mad Men*–mania: there's also been a loving embrace of the era's boudoir-licious intimates—which has, of course, spilled over into today's retro styles. That reigning '60s screen stars Elizabeth Taylor and Claudia Cardinale played some of their most memorable scenes in lacy chemises and push-up bras reminds us of pre-feminist days when a women's sphere of influence was more bedroom than boardroom. Thankfully, we've come a long way, but no harm in a lingering affection for the lingerie.

Left to right: Claudia Cardinale as Elena in *The Hell with Heroes*; Elizabeth Taylor plays a call girl in *BUtterfield 8*; Eva Mendes is the Other Woman in *The Women*; Anne Bancroft, the über cougar in *The Graduate*; January Jones in *X-Men: First Class*; and Sienna Miller as Edie Sedgwick in *Factory Girl*.

FASHION'S INTERNAL AFFAIRS

What we see on the runway doesn't often translate literally to reality; but the big themes do resonate. Lingerie-as-outerwear burst on the scene in the '90s, when Madonna toured in Jean Paul Gaultier's infamous cone bra and corset and has refused to quit the stage. While new variations are more demure than dominatrix—with softer lines, looser shapes, more delicate materials—there's plenty left of the signature subversiveness and daring. How to make it work to flatter your figure? Like bare skin, sheer lingerie fabrics will always distract the eye so you control what people focus on and what they don't. A completely crushworthy see-through lace dress acts as one louche layer over very visible high-waisted (and tummy-taming) panties. Depending on the occasion and your comfort level, a big, swingy overcoat tops it all off and softens the impact. It's about balancing the bare with something substantial and making a big statement with the unmentionable.

See right through A silk cami with chiffon overlay sexes up a pencil skirt.

Pro tulle
A black tulle midi discreetly distracts from visible lace panties.

Chiffon chic
Shocking? So not: it covers no more or less than what you'd wear at the beach.

Lacy fair
A roomy overcoat allows you the option of covering up, or not.

The lingerie
designer grew
her business to
include shapewear:
"Be relevant to
the changing
customer," says
Josie Natori.

Ask Josie

(The soft-wear mogul on remolding style.)

Wall Streeter-turned designer Josie Natori discusses the value of underpinnings and why she's banking on shapewear.

SHE WAS MERRILL LYNCH'S FIRST-EVER FEMALE VP of investment banking who went on to build an empire on exquisite lingerie, yet Josie Natori admits, "Good enough is never good enough." Not only did she expand into home fragrance, eyewear, and ready-to-wear, she dove headfirst into the burgeoning shapewear market. "Be relevant to the changing customer!" Natori said, and knowing well the evolving aesthetics and consumer demands of the culture—and that a reported 80 percent of women wear the wrong bra size—Natori couldn't resist jumping in to help reshape the world.

You've shared that lingerie is the "starting point of what you wear every day." Is it fair to say that's not the case for most women? What are the consequences for not taking lingerie seriously, say, when you're wearing something clingy and revealing?

JN: Inner and outwear should always work as a team. If the occasion calls for a crisp white blouse and wide-leg black pants, you've got a totally opaque tailored look, which lends itself to something dramatic, you can have fun with feather lace appliqués. But a skin-hugging jersey dress requires smoothing underthings that contain curves while effecting a natural-looking shape—a full-coverage bra with a little padding and a thong that sits low on your hips and is virtually invisible.

What is the ideal lingerie for sheer fabrics?

JN: There are lots of contouring and smooth-curve bras with semisheer yet supportive fabrics that lift without bulkiness. For stretchy skirts or shorts, you'll want an ultrasmooth brief with elastic shirring that sits just below the natural waist and guarantees no visible panty line.

Is it better to just go bra-less if you're wearing strapless?

JN: On the contrary, if you're wearing a strapless gown—which usually means it's a formal affair—you're going to need extra reinforcement in your bra. Plastic boning in the side seams and lightweight padding will give a more natural look. It's all about the fabrics, and power mesh and spandex get the job done without any squeezing or discomfort.

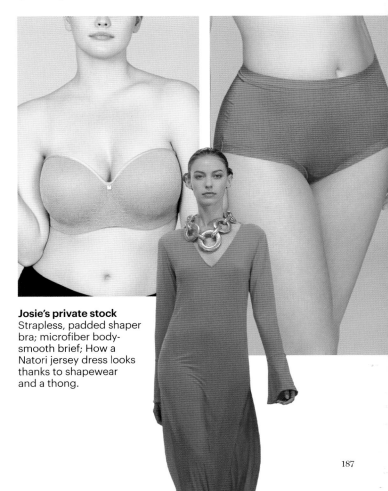

Josie's private stock
Strapless, padded shaper bra; microfiber body-smooth brief; How a Natori jersey dress looks thanks to shapewear and a thong.

GREAT SHAPES

"My saddlebags are why Spanx exists," declared Sara Blakely, founder of the shapewear company that revolutionized fashion's "under" world. Asked for specifics, she added, "I didn't like the way I looked in a pair of white pants." For her it's pants, for the next girl it could be a tank top that gave away her muffin top. Whatever: A demand for underwear that would give women a slimmer shapelier look has been met by an endless supply of new foundation wear. Panties that lift and separate your butt, high-waisted thigh-slimmers, and tummy-control bodysuits that also bring up the rear. Shapewear, wherever you wear it, is your point of depature for every great look.

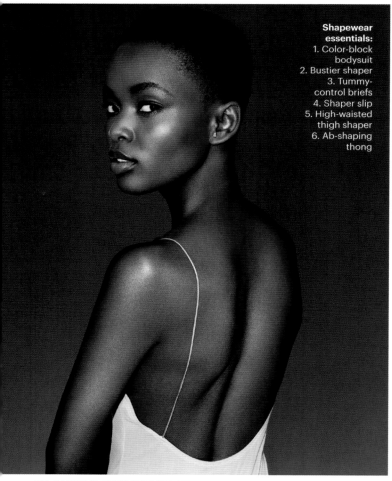

Shapewear essentials:
1. Color-block bodysuit
2. Bustier shaper
3. Tummy-control briefs
4. Shaper slip
5. High-waisted thigh shaper
6. Ab-shaping thong

photo credits

COVER: Tesh

BACK COVER: Yu Tsai

PAGE 4: Isabel Asha Penzlien

PAGE 6: Mark Abrahams

PAGE 8: Alexander Tamargo/Getty Images

PAGES 10-11, CLOCKWISE FROM TOP LEFT: Courtesy Everett Collection; David Seymour/Magnum Photos; Amy Graves/WireImage; Jon Kopaloff/FilmMagic; Gotcha Images/Splash News

PAGES 12-13, CLOCKWISE FROM TOP LEFT: Mark Lim; Dan Lecca; Markus Pritzi; Paul Archuleta/FilmMagic; Steve Granitz/WireImage. Stills: Studio D

PAGES 14-15, FROM LEFT: Universal International Pictures/The Kobal Collection; Universal/Courtesy Everett Collection; HBO/Courtesy Everett Collection; Courtesy Everett Collection. Stills: Studio D

PAGES 16-17, CLOCKWISE FROM LEFT: Charles Eshelman/FilmMagic; Gareth Cuttermole/Getty Images; Vince Bucci/NBCU/Getty; Steve Granitz/WireImage; Jeffrey Mayer/WireImage; Mike Marsland/Wireimage

PAGES 18-19, FROM LEFT: Jon Shearer/WireImage; Charles Gallay/Getty Images; Pascal Le Segretain/Getty Images; Jeffrey Mayer/WireImage; Kevin Mazur/WireImage

PAGES 20-21, FROM LEFT: CR7/Splash News; Catwalking/Getty Images; MGM/Courtesy Neal Peters Collection; Elina Kechicheva. Stills: Studio D

PAGES 22-23, FROM LEFT: Dan Lecca (3); Victor Virgile/Getty Images

PAGES 24-25, CLOCKWISE FROM BOTTOM LEFT: Paul Morigi/WireImage; Jacopo Rayle/Getty Images; Karl-Edwin Guerre (4)

PAGES 26-27, FROM LEFT: Regan Cameron; Jeffrey Mayer/WireImage; Jon Kopaloff/FimMagic; Michael Kovac/FilmMagic; Kevin Mazur/WireImage; Jason Kempin/Getty Images; Steve Granitz/WireImage; Frazer Harrison/Getty Images; Lester Cohen/WireImage; Mike Marsland/WireImage

PAGES 28-29, FROM LEFT: Neil Kirk; Heidi Levine/Getty Images; Dan Lecca; Charles Eshelman/FilmMagic

PAGE 30: Alex Cayley

PAGE 32-33, CLOCKWISE FROM TOP LEFT: Rex USA/Everett Collection; CBS/Getty Images; Vittorio Zunino Celotto/Getty Images; Samir Hussein/Getty Images; Michael Stewart/WireImage

PAGES 34-35, CLOCKWISE FROM TOP LEFT: Silja Magg; Dan Lecca; Danilo Giuliani; Steve Granitz/WireImage. Stills: Studio D

PAGES 36-37, FROM LEFT: Dan Lecca (5). Stills: Studio D

PAGES 38-39, CLOCKWISE FROM LEFT: Dan Lecca; Tesh; Dan Lecca. Stills: Studio D

PAGES 40-41 CLOCKWISE FROM LEFT: Steve Granitz/WireImage; Jon Kopaloff/FilmMagic; Vittorio Zunino Celotto/Getty Images; George Pimentel/WireImage; Jeffrey Mayer/WireImage; Jason LaVeris/FilmMagic

PAGES 42-43, FROM LEFT: AKM GSI; Gabriel Olsen/Getty Images; Antonio de Moraes Barros Filho/WireImage; Paul J. Richards/AFP/Getty Images

PAGES 44-45, FROM LEFT: Warner Bros./Courtesy of Everett Collection; Hulton Archive/Getty Images; Dreamworks/Everett Collection; 20th Century Fox/Everett Collection. Stills: Studio D

PAGES 46-47, CLOCKWISE FROM LEFT: Karl-Edwin Guerre; Greg Kessler; Mark Lim (2); Greg Kessler; Mark Lim

PAGES 48-49: Dan Lecca (4)

PAGES 50-51, FROM LEFT: Gomillion and Leupols/Contour by Getty Images; Pascal Le Segretain/Getty Images; Jordan Strauss/WireImage; Kevin Winter/Getty Images; Jim Spellman/WireImage; Steve Granitz/WireImage; D Dipasupil/FilmMagic; C Flanigan/Getty Images; John Shearer/WireImage

PAGES 52-53, FROM LEFT: Tesh; Dave M. Benett/Getty Images; Donato Sardella/WireImage; Dan Lecca

PAGE 54: Jan Welters

PAGES 56-57, CLOCKWISE FROM TOP LEFT: Hulton Archive/Getty Images; Hammer/The Kobal Collection; Lisa Marie Williams/Getty Images; Dave M. Benett/Getty Images; Jeffrey Mayer/WireImage

PAGES 58-59, FROM LEFT: Angeru Zerita; Venturelli/WireImage; Andrew H. Walker/Getty Images; Tony Kim. Stills: Studio D

PAGES 60-61: Dan Lecca (3). Stills: Studio D

PAGES 62-63, FROM LEFT: Dan Lecca; Evening Standard/Getty Images; Dan Lecca; David Roemer. Stills: Studio D

PAGES 64-65, FROM LEFT: Jean Baptiste Lacroix/WireImage; 20th Century Fox Film Corp./Everett Collection; Pichichi/Splash News. Stills: Studio D

PAGES 66-67: Dan Lecca (5)

PAGES 68-69, CLOCKWISE FROM LEFT: Adam Katz Sinding (2); Mark Lim; Frazer Harrison/WireImage; Mark Lim; Timur Emek/Getty Images

PAGES 70-71, FROM LEFT: Clint Brewer/Splash News; David Parker/Getty; Michael Tran/FilmMagic; Jason LaVeris/FilmMagic; Johns PKI/Splash News; Alo Ceballos/FilmMagic

PAGES 72-73, FROM LEFT: Courtesy of the Designer; Catwalking/Getty Images; Jeffrey Mayer/WireImage; Amy Sussman/Getty Images

PAGE 74: Danilo Giuliani

PAGES 76-77, CLOCKWISE FROM TOP LEFT: The Print Collector/Getty Images; Keystone-France/Gamma-Keystone via Getty Images; Michael N. Todaro/FilmMagic; Bob Thomas/Getty Images; Steve Granitz/WireImage

PAGES 78-79, CLOCKWISE FROM TOP LEFT: Jason Lloyd-Evans; Markus Pritzi; Astrid Munoz/Getty Images; Jemal Countess/Getty Images. Stills: Studio D

PAGES 80-81, FROM LEFT: Francois Campos; Courtesy of the Designer; Dan Lecca; Courtesy of the Designer. Stills: Studio D

PAGES 82-83, FROM LEFT: Dan Lecca; Boe Marion; Dan Lecca; Tommy Ton/Trunk Archive. Stills: Studio D

PAGES 84-85, FROM LEFT: Dan Lecca; Jason Llyod-Evans; Catwalking/Getty Images; Dan Lecca (2). Stills: Studio D

PAGES 86-87, FROM LEFT: Solimene Photography/Getty Images; Jon Kopaloff/Getty Images; Steve Granitz/WireImage; China Foto Press/Getty Images; George Pimentel/WireImage; Dimitrios Kambouris/WireImage

PAGES 88-89, FROM LEFT: Steven Lovekin/FilmMagic; Kevin Mazur/WireImage (2); Jason LaVeris/FilmMagic

PAGES 90-91, FROM LEFT: 20th Century Fox Film Corp./Courtesy Everett Collection; Bridge Lane Library/Popperfoto/Getty Images; Dimension Films/Everett Collection; 20th Century Fox/Paramount/Kobal Collection. Stills: Studio D

PAGES 92-93: Dan Lecca (4)

PAGES 94-95, CLOCKWISE FROM TOP LEFT: Silvia Olsen; Stockholm Street Style; Bek Andersen; Mark Lim; Bek Andersen (2)

PAGES 96-97, FROM LEFT: Satoshi Saikusa; Kevin Mazur/WireImage; Dimitrios Kambouris/WireImage; Gregg DeGuire/WireImage; Charles Eshleman/FilmMagic; Jason LaVeris/FilmMagic; Kevin Mazur/WireImage; Gregg DeGuire/WireImage; Jun Sato/WireImage

PAGES 98-99, FROM LEFT: Tesh; Dan Lecca; Getty Images; Dimitrios Kambouris/Getty Images

PAGE 100: Andrew Yee

PAGES 102-103, CLOCKWISE FROM TOP LEFT: Mary Evans/Columbia Pictures/Ronald Grant/Everett Collection; Paramount/The Kobal Collection; Larry Busaca/Getty Images; Trae Patton/NBCU Photobank; Jason Merritt/Getty Images

PAGES 104-105, FROM LEFT: Mark Lim; Meredith Jenks; Kevin Mazur/WireImage; Alex Cayley. Stills: Studio D

PAGES 106-107, FROM LEFT: Thomas Nutzl; Pascal Le Segretain/Getty Images; Dan Leca (2); Richard Bard/Getty Images. Stills: Studio D

PAGES 108-109, FROM LEFT: Markus Pritzi; Dan Lecca (2). Stills: Studio D

PAGES 110-111, FROM LEFT: New Line Cinema/The Kobal Collection; Carol Co/The Kobal Collection; Sam Emerson/MGM/The Kobal Collection; Paramount/Courtesy of Everett Collection. Stills: Studio D

PAGES 112-113, CLOCKWISE FROM LEFT: Chris Weeks/WireImage; Brooks/INF photo; FR Photos/Splash News; Jennifer Mitchell/Splash News; PSD/Splash News; JB Nicholas/Splash News/Corbis; Aik Arshamion/INF photo

PAGE 114-115, FROM LEFT: Dan Lecca (3); Pascal Le Segretain/Getty Images

PAGE 116-117, CLOCKWISE FROM LEFT: Stephania Yarni/Text Styles; Mark Lim (5)

PAGE 118-119, FROM LEFT: Tesh; Gregg DeGuire/WireImage; Desiree Navarro/WireImage; Jeffrey Mayer/WireImage (2); Kevin Winter/Getty Images; Nathaniel Jones/Pacific Coast News; Gregg DeGuire/WireImage

PAGES 120-121, CLOCKWISE FROM LEFT: Courtesy of the Designer; Splash News (2); Frazer Harrison/Getty Images; INF Photo; Tomasso Boddi/WireImage

PAGE 122: Enrique Badulescu

PAGE 124-125, CLOCKWISE FROM TOP LEFT: Everett Collection (2); INF Photo; Ray Tamara/Getty Images; Shawaf Grimes/Pacific Coast News

PAGE 126-127, CLOCKWISE FROM BOTTOM LEFT: Starsurf/Stewy/Splash News; Splash News (2); Desiree Navarro/FilmMagic; Clint Brewer/Splash News; TC/Splash News

PAGE 128-129, CLOCKWISE FROM TOP LEFT: Courtesy of the Designer (4). Stills: Studio D

PAGE 130-131, FROM LEFT: Courtesy of the Designer (2)

PAGE 132: Enrique Badulescu

PAGE 134-135, CLOCKWISE FROM TOP LEFT: Silver Screen Collection/Getty Images; GAB Archives/Redferns; Jeffrey Mayer/WireImage; Buzz Foto/FilmMagic; Kevin Mazur/WireImage

PAGE 136-137, CLOCKWISE FROM TOP LEFT: Dan Monick; Dan Lecca (2); Thomas Nutzl. Stills: Studio D

PAGE 138-139, FROM LEFT: Dan Lecca (5). Stills: Studio D

PAGE 140-141, CLOCKWISE FROM TOP LEFT: Kristen Sinclair/Getty Images; Caroline McCredie/Getty Images (3); Kristen Sinclair/Getty Images; Timur Emek/Getty Images; Adam Katz Sinding; Caroline McCredie/Getty Images; Kristen Sinclair/Getty Images (3)

PAGES 142-143, CLOCKWISE FROM LEFT: Jerritt Clark/WireImage; Pierre Syu/FilmMagic; Larry Busacca/Getty Image; Splash News; Dominique Charriau/Wire Image; Karwai/FilmMagic; Dominique Charriau/WireImage

PAGE 144-145, FROM LEFT: Richard Pierce. Stills: Studio D

PAGES 146-147, FROM LEFT: Dan Lecca (7). Stills: Studio D

PAGES 148-149, CLOCKWISE FROM LEFT: Caroline McCredie/Getty Images; Karl-Edwin Guerre; Frazer Harrison/Getty Images; Adam Katz Sinding; Caroline McCredie/Getty Images; Caroline McCredie/Getty Images; Jessica Weber/Blaublut Edition; Mark Lim; Timur Emek/Getty Images

PAGES 150-151, CLOCKWISE FROM TOP LEFT: PPNY/GSNY/Splash News; KCS Presse/Splash News; Larry Busacca/Getty Images (3); Weir Photos/Splash News; Donatto Sardella/WireImage; Gotcha Images/Splash News

PAGES 152-153, FROM LEFT: Tony Kim. Stills: Studio D

PAGES 154-155, CLOCKWISE FROM TOP LEFT: Larry Busacca/Getty Images; Jeff Kravitz/WireImage; John Shearer/WireImage; James Devaney/GC Images; Larry Busacca/Getty Images; Valerie Macon/AFP/Getty Images; Michel Dufour/Getty Images; Rob Kim/Getty Images; Steve Granitz/WireImage

PAGES 156-157, FROM LEFT: Ron Asadorian/Splash News; Jason Meritt/Getty Images; Steve Granitz/WireImage; Michael Buckner/Getty Images; Larry Busacca/Getty Images

PAGES 158-159: Dan Lecca (8)

PAGES 160-161, FROM LEFT: Matt Jones. Stills: Studio D

PAGES 162-163, CLOCKWISE FROM TOP LEFT: Dan Lecca; Santi/Splash News; Jacopo Raule/FilmMagic; Splash News; Santi/Splash News; DVT/Star Max/FilmMagic. Stills: Studio D

PAGES 164-165, FROM LEFT: Tesh; Catwalking/Getty Images

PAGES 166-167, CLOCKWISE FROM LEFT: Dominique Charriau/WireImage; Catwalking/Getty Images; Stefanie Keenan/Getty Images; Victor Virgile/Gamma-Rapho via Getty Images; Donato Sardella/WireImage; Catwalking/Getty Images; Jason Llyod-Evans; Catwalking/Getty Images

PAGE 168: Danilo Giuliani

PAGES 170-171, CLOCKWISE FROM TOP LEFT: Columbia/Kobal Collection; CCC/Concordia/The Kobal Collection; Miramax/Courtesy Everett Collection; Andreas Otero/Everett Collection; Michael Underwood/Getty Images

PAGES 172-173, FROM LEFT: Wendelien Daan; Dan Lecca; Tesh. Stills: Studio D

PAGES 174-175, FROM RIGHT: Alex Cayley. Stills: Studio D

PAGES 176-177, FROM LEFT: Fabio Chizzola. Stills: Studio D

PAGES 178-179, FROM LEFT: Michael Loccisano/FilmMagic; George Pimentel/WireImage; Kevin Mazur/WireImage; Steve Grantiz/WireImage; Victor Chavez/WireImage; Jon Kopaloff/FilmMagic

PAGES 180-181, FROM LEFT: Jason LaVeris/FilmMagic; Michael Kovac/WireImage; Jesse Grant/Getty Images; Jeff Kravitz/WireImage

PAGES 182-183, CLOCKWISE FROM LEFT: Universal/The Kobal Collection; Courtesy Everett Collection; Jagged Films/Picturehouse/Kobal Collection; Embassy/Laurence Turman/The Kobal Collection; Weinstein Company/Courtesy Everett Collection; Murray Close/TM and 20th Century Fox Film Corp./Courtesy Everett Collection

PAGES 184-185: Dan Lecca (4)

PAGES 186-187: Courtesy of the Designer (4)

PAGES 188-189, FROM LEFT: Patric Shaw; Wendelien Daan. Stills: Studio D